SURVIVAL NOTES
FOR RACE FANS

SURVIVAL NOTES
FOR RACE FANS

INSPIRATION FOR THE
DRIVE THROUGH LIFE

BY
ROBERT STOFEL

Ambassador
Books
New York/Mahwah, NJ

Book and cover design by Jennifer Conlan
Cover photo by Patrick Schneider

Library of Congress Cataloging-in-Publication Data

Stofel, Robert, 1962-
  Survival notes for race fans : inspiration for the drive through life
/ by Robert Stofel.
     p. cm.
  ISBN 978-0-8091-4646-8 (alk. paper)
  1. Sports spectators--Religious life. 2. Motor sports--Miscellanea.
I. Title.
  BV4596.A87S76 2010
  242--dc22
                                    2009046242
Published by Ambassador Books
An imprint of Paulist Press
997 Macarthur Boulevard
Mahwah, New Jersey 07430

www.ambassadorbooks.com

Printed and bound in the United States of America

*To my father and brother
who taught me to love NASCAR
as much as they do*

CONTENTS

INTRODUCTION

At the age of eight I grasped the fence at Talladega watching Bobby Isaac, Darrell Waltrip, the Allison brothers, and King Richard Petty battling it out around the 2.66-mile track. This was back in the day when a child could get close to the fence and not have to worry about being chased away by a policeman. And I stood there with my fingers clenching the fence the way a bird grips a power line, watching the action while my father sat behind me in the grandstands. I was accustomed to attending Saturday night racing at the Nashville Fairgrounds, but going to Talladega was different. The pack of cars would roar by and disappear around turn four, and then they would come rushing off turn two and down the backstretch. You could eat a hotdog before they rounded the track. And we were too poor to buy tickets for the frontstretch, so we huddled with the marginalized and the people who loved racing as much as they did their beer. And we hollered, waved our ball caps, and whistled with reverence at the pack of cars as if our cheering would make them go faster. If our favorite driver wrecked or blew an engine, we'd slump in our seats as if all hope in the world went with them into the garage area.

A lot has changed in NASCAR over the years. A kid can no longer clench the fence and feel the rush of wind on his face. Admission prices have skyrocketed. The cars are faster and more sophisticated. The wrecks seem more violent. But our love for NASCAR hasn't changed. We still cheer and whistle at the pack of cars as they roar around the speedway, but the cheers are louder. Attendance has grown astronomically since the 1970s, and my love for motorsports hasn't waned. So writing this book was a labor of love and passion.

Survival Notes for Race Fans are devotionals that take the reader inside the world of NASCAR to find inspiration for the sacred race of life. Gently drawing upon the race-of-life metaphor, each devotional ties the spiritual life with some aspect of motorsports, and each devotional has a quote from drivers, crew chiefs, and other diplomats of racing. The result is a power-packed devotional book that will lift your soul and have you roaring into the race of each daily grind. Enjoy!

I have fought the good fight,
I have finished the race,
I have kept the faith.
— *Timothy 4:7*

No discipline seems pleasant at the time, but painful. Later on, however, it produces a harvest of righteousness and peace for those who have been trained by it.

— Hebrews 12:11

ONE

BEFORE THE GREEN FLAG DROPS

Before the green flag ever drops at a racetrack, engineers and mechanics pour over every inch of the racecar. They run mechanical tests. Each racecar is taken to the wind tunnel to determine the drag. A fast racecar is an aerodynamic racecar. Optimum performance goes into every car before it reaches the track. Preparation is the key to victory.

The same is true for our spiritual life. We must prepare. Spiritual discipline will help us grow our relationship with God. Each moment we spend in prayer, in solitude, in reading the Holy Scriptures, the closer we get to Christ. And if you long to be more like Christ, then learn to prepare your heart. Take a moment each day, and ask God to fill you with his presence. It's always a good way to prepare before the green flag of the day drops. Then discipline yourself to do this each day. Soul preparation is the key to having a great day no matter what the day may bring.

First you learn to drive fast. Next, you learn to drive fast in traffic. Then, you learn how to do it for 500 miles.
— *Alan Kulwicki*

A man's steps are directed by the LORD. How then can anyone understand his own way?

— *Proverbs 20:24*

TWO

"START YOUR ENGINES!"

"Start your engines" is the most famous phrase in NASCAR. It gets crazy after this. The noise is deafening. Adrenaline is coursing through our veins. It's time to put every moment of waiting into gear. We don't know how the race will unfold. Will our driver win? Will he wreck? Will he get muddled down in the middle of the pack? We never know what a race holds for them, so we must watch, wait, and hope.

Waiting and hoping play big roles in our lives. Sometimes our lives start strong, and then things don't work out the way we planned. We wreck our careers. We total our marriages or maybe just the fenders get bent. It's hard to know how our lives will finish once we start them, but love, hope, and faith are simply and romantically what hold the fibers of our future together. Keep these three ahead of you, and you'll finish strong.

> I'm kind of quiet but when I put my helmet on,
> it's like you flip a switch. I'm ready to go.
> — *Martin Truex Jr.*

*T*he LORD had said to Abram, "Leave your country, your people and your father's household and go to the land I will show you."

— *Genesis 12:1*

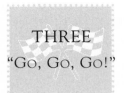

THREE

"Go, Go, Go!"

When the green flag drops, every spotter yells, "Green, green, green!" into their driver's radio, letting them know that the race has begun. This is a spotter's job. They are the eyes high above when the driver gets lost in the pack.

In a sense, God told Abraham, "Green, green, green"—to go into the land he would show him. So Abraham obeyed. He went, not knowing where he was going. At some point, we will hear the call to leave all behind and follow Christ because Christ is still saying, "Come, follow me." And maybe the difference between Abraham and us is the way God said, "Go" to him and Christ says, "Come, follow me" to us. Following is better than going. Going is like heading into the great unknown, unsure of what awaits us. Following is staying in the shadow of the Cross, living by Christ's example. It's obeying the sacred call and letting go of the desire to control our life. This is what it means to follow.

It's go time. We need to score points, a lot of points, every race.
— *Jimmie Johnson*

*T*hen the angel said to me, "Write: 'Blessed are those who are invited to the wedding supper of the Lamb!' " And he added, "These are the true words of God."

— *Revelation 19:9*

ROBERT STOFEL

FOUR
Pre-Race Festivities

Pre-race festivities are either annoying or enjoyable to drivers. Some drivers would probably rather see the green flag than a flyover by jets. They want to get the show started. Others revel in being interviewed. They love the bands, the singing of the national anthem, and the way the pit crews line up on pit road. To them, it's a festival.

Heaven will be like pre-race festivities. There will be singing and angel flyovers. The Lord loves a great celebration. When the prodigal son returned, the father said, "Kill the fatted calf. Let's party. My son is home." Jesus even said, "The kingdom of heaven is like a king who prepared a wedding banquet for his son." So there will be rejoicing at the wedding supper of the Lamb. Until then, let us sing his praises. We might as well get ready. The banquet is being prepared. So hear the Lord: "Come to the wedding banquet" (Matt 22:4). Answer God's invitation. Open your life to him today.

Today races are won with what you bring to the track . . . and the car has to be ready to go. And if it's not, you can't fix it at the racetrack anymore.

— *Jeff Burton*

*T*his calls for patient endurance and faithfulness on the part of the saints.

— *Revelation 13:10*

ROBERT STOFEL

FIVE

TAKE SOME TAPE OFF

*T*eams tape the front grills to restrict the wind, to make it flow over the car instead of through the grill. It makes the car faster. But too much tape will cause the car to overheat. This is why teams limit tape use during a long race. But during qualifying, most teams tape the grills completely, so the cars will travel faster.

Think of yourself as the grill of a racecar. There will be times when you will need no air. The distance is short. Speed is what you want. So accomplish your task. Make peace with someone. Do the chore. Finish the project. Don't belabor the point.

Yet there will be times when you will need to prepare for an endurance race. So pace yourself. Take some tape off. Breathe a little bit. You have time. Make it easier on yourself. Trying to accomplish too much, too fast will overheat your capacities. You'll give out from exhaustion. So today, maybe you are in something for the long haul. Don't get restless. Stay smart. Endure until the end.

Once you try to do more than your equipment is capable of doing,
you get yourself in trouble, and you start wrecking.
— *Dale Jarrett*

*B*rothers, stop thinking like children. In regard to evil be infants, but in your thinking be adults.

— *1 Corinthians 14:20*

SIX
THE ROOKIE STRIPE

In NASCAR, rookies are identified with yellow stripes on their back bumpers. It's like a warning sign that says, "I don't know everything yet. I haven't raced on all of the tracks, so be careful, I'm prone to make mistakes."

Every human being should have a rookie stripe. We're prone to make mistakes. We have much to learn and will continue to learn until we die. But we should never use the rookie stripe as an excuse to continue making mistakes.

The rookie stripe is good for one season. The second season a driver is considered a veteran. He's raced all of the tracks. He's made rookie mistakes, but it is all behind him now. The yellow stripe is gone. There will come a day when your rookie season will end. Your mistakes will be behind you. You will be better prepared. So move on. Things will get easier if you don't give up.

> As a rookie, every place is challenging!
> You have to learn what each track needs.
> — *Kurt Busch*

*T*hen Jesus came to them and said, "All authority in heaven and on earth has been given to me."

— *Matthew 28:18*

SEVEN
ONE OF THOSE RACING DEALS

We hear it all the time in racing. A wreck occurs, and when it is clearly no one's fault, we call it, "One of those racing deals."

Why do racing deals happen? They're like what insurance companies call "acts of God"—random and senseless. But natural occurrences in a fallen world are not God's fault. Sure, he left the door open to the possibility of bad things. But he did so for free will to exist. Sometimes we feel like God is against us, especially if a tornado rips through our house. We think God is punishing us. But there are racing deals in life. Sure, God has all authority, but he doesn't dictate free will. No one is to blame for what has happened. It is what it is. The great thing about failure in a race is the opportunity to race again next week. So don't question God. Call it "one of those racing deals" and move forward.

It was just one of those racing deals, you know. I wanted to come down behind him, and I just misjudged and clipped him there.
— *David Gilliland*

Now you are the body of Christ, and each one of you is a part of it.

— *1 Corinthians 12:27*

EIGHT

The Race Is Won or Lost on Pit Road

*T*he race is won or lost on pit road. One stumble, one dropped lug nut, one miscue of any kind, and you can lose your spot on the track. This is why so much work goes into building teamwork. It matters.

We are only as successful as those we put around us. "Do not be misled: Bad company corrupts good character" (1 Cor 15:33). Successful pit crews have the right people in the correct places. As Christians, we should be great at teamwork. Look around you today. What kind of pit crew have you assembled? If you were a racecar driver, would they help you win? Are you losing? Do you have the right jack man—someone who will lift you when you are down? Do you have the right tire carriers—people who will help you share the load? Do you have the right crew chief—someone who will help you make the right calls?

> Teamwork is everything. It takes all of us working together.
> We win and lose together.
> *— Jeff Gordon*

*T*urn from your evil ways, and stop all your evil practices.

— *Zechariah 1:4*

NINE
CHECKING UP

Drivers check up. They slowdown abruptly. They hit the brakes to avoid wrecks. At other times, they check up to keep from wrecking themselves. And it is always dangerous to check up on a racetrack. The drivers behind you will run over you. Without brake lights, it's hard to tell when other drivers hit their brakes. It's sudden. This is why there are so many secondary wrecks due to primary ones. They just can't tell when a car in front checks up.

There are times when we need to check up. We need to stop our abrupt anger, stop our lusting, stop our greed. We need to stop allowing sin to get the best of us. So check up. Stop. Take a moment to clear your head. Count to ten. Think of how this sin might affect your future. Play it out to the end inside your mind. Then decide if it is worth it.

The wall always wins.
— *Boris Said*

*T*herefore confess your sins to each other and pray for each other so that you may be healed. The prayer of a righteous man is powerful and effective.

— *James 5:16*

TEN
SPOTTERS

Spotters make drivers safer and more competitive. They are the eyes in the back of a driver's head. They see the whole track. Every wreck, every turn of action.

"Inside."

"Three-wide."

"Everyone is single file."

"Go high."

"Got one looking inside."

"Pit this time by."

And the list goes on. Spotters warn of wrecks. They tell drivers when to pit. They speak at all the right junctures and keep drivers from becoming islands on the racetrack.

Do you have someone who can speak into your life? Maybe someone who can see your blind spots? We all need a spotter, so if you don't have such a person, find one. Then confess one to the other.

> It is amazing what can be accomplished when
> nobody cares about who gets the credit.
> — *Robert Yates*

*T*hat is why, for Christ's sake, I delight in weaknesses, in insults, in hardships, in persecutions, in difficulties. For when I am weak, then I am strong.

— 2 Corinthians 12:10

ELEVEN
SCUFFED TIRES

*T*eams will sometimes scuff in a set of tires during practice. They will run the new set of sticker tires for a few laps and scuff the newness from them. They will heat them up, then let them cool, which will change the characteristics of the tire, making it harder.

It doesn't seem logical to race on used tires. New always sounds better. But scuffed tires can give the car better traction and, under certain circumstances, make the car faster.

Think of your life as a set of scuffed tires. Maybe you feel worn-out. Maybe you feel used. Maybe you look around at the young and think you're old. Maybe you don't function as well as you once did. But if you think of scuffed tires in a positive way, then your weakness can make you stronger. For God's power is made perfect in weakness. This is the paradox of scuffed tires. Used in the right situation, with the power of God, we are better weak than strong. God loves to use a set of scuffed tires.

I prefer never to be on stickers.
— *Dale Earnhardt Jr.*

One who was there had been an invalid for thirty-eight years. When Jesus saw him lying there and learned that he had been in this condition for a long time, he asked him, "Do you want to get well?"

— John 5:5–6

TWELVE
LUCKY DOG

*T*he first car that is down a lap receives the Lucky Dog when a caution comes out. It's his free pass. It puts him back on the lead lap. But it is never based solely on luck. This is why drivers keep digging and keep putting themselves into position to receive the Lucky Dog. A lot of hard work is involved. A driver has to position himself to receive it. He must be the first car a lap down when the caution comes out.

Take the man at the pool of Bethesda. For thirty-eight years, he put himself in position to receive a healing. For thirty-eight years, he lay beside the pool crippled because he had no one to carry him to the water when the angel stirred it. But he never gave up.

So keep doing the right thing. Keep positioning yourself for a blessing. It may take thirty-eight years, or it could happen today. Are you ready? Are you in position?

We just need some luck, however I can get that. I don't know.
There's not a store where you can go buy that.
— *Dale Earnhardt Jr.*

F*or God is not a God of disorder but of peace.*

— 1 Corinthians 14:33

THIRTEEN

RESTRICTOR-PLATE RACING

Restrictor-plate racing breeds the Big One—the multiple car wreck that becomes spectacular fireworks with cars smashing into one another, lighting up the sky like fabulous Roman candles. Because one misstep at speeds over 190 m.p.h. means the Big One. So why require teams to run a restrictor plate? Because restrictor plates have smaller holes for air intake and slow the cars down; otherwise, the cars could become airborne and fly into the grandstands. But no one is denying the danger in which it places the drivers. So there is no easy answer to restrictor-plate racing.

When we face the problem of pain and suffering in the world, there seems to be no easy answer, either. The world is a dangerous place. Evil can get the best of us. We can get caught up in the Big One—the evil outcome of someone else's sin. It doesn't make sense. Doesn't seem fair. But free will is better than the other option, which is becoming a robot, becoming what we were never meant to be.

I'm not a robot; I have a personality and I have emotions.
I have a humorous side to me and an angry side to me.
— *Jeff Gordon*

*L*et us throw off everything that hinders and the sin that so easily entangles, and let us run with perseverance the race marked out for us.

— *Hebrews 12:1*

FOURTEEN
THE ONE THING

Every engineer who works on the car, every pit crew member, every owner, every driver wants one thing—the win. They want the checkered flag and the trophy. They want to finish first.

What is your one thing? What do you want above everything? For King David's men it was to get their commander a drink of water from the well in Jericho. Nehemiah wanted to rebuild the ruined wall around Jerusalem. For the Apostle Paul it was to put the past behind him. For Jesus it was the Cross.

If you knew you had only one year left to live, what would change? What would be your one thing? Children? A career? A certain relationship? Becoming like Christ?

The race of our life has been marked out for us. Our years on earth may be long or short. So we must throw off everything that hinders our race and focus our energy on the one thing, which Christ says should be the kingdom of God (Matt 6:33).

> For us there is no difference between second
> and tenth, it's win or nothing.
> — *Denny Hamlin*

*I*f we confess our sins, he is faithful and just and will forgive us our sins and purify us from all unrighteousness.

— 1 John 1:9

FIFTEEN

TEAROFFS

*B*ack in the day, crews washed driver's windshields with a long squeegee during a pit stop, similar to the way we wash our windshields at gas stations. But these days teams have tearoffs, which are clear layers of plastic that can be ripped off during pit stops, removing dirt from the windshields.

Confession is much like a tearoff. It removes sin that has dirtied our souls, leaving us with a better view of God.

David used a tearoff in Psalm 51. "Wash away all my iniquity and cleanse me from my sin" (v. 2). He had muddied things up by having an affair with Bathsheba. Then he killed her husband to cover it up. Then came the moment when he realized his sin. This was when he penned Psalm 51. Take a moment to read it today. Then confess your own sins. It will keep things clear. You will get a better view of God.

Sometimes I say things I shouldn't, and it's not a good feeling. But the good feeling is knowing that I can always go to God in prayer and confess and say, "I know I'm doing wrong. Help me because I don't know how to fix it."

— *David Reutimann*

My soul thirsts for God, for the living God. When can I go and meet with God?

— *Psalm 42:2*

SIXTEEN
THE DRIVERS' MEETING

*T*he drivers' meeting takes place before the race. Usually officials will discuss rule changes or remind drivers of certain rules for individual tracks. And every drivers' meeting is mandatory. Drivers who miss this meeting must start at the rear of the field, forfeiting their qualifying position.

Every Christian should start the day with a drivers' meeting. We should pray about the coming day, and then listen. We can pray for direction or for the sick, the poor, the bereaved. But we must never think we are too busy to meet with God. We will forfeit the power and peace that is ours in Christ Jesus.

In Psalm 42:2, the psalmist's soul needed nourishment. He needed time with God to draw upon God's strength. So take a few moments today, and thirst for God. Ask him to water the dry places in your soul and give you strength for today's race.

> I found out in life that if you pay attention,
> God will give you a direction.
> — *Morgan Shepherd*

Be strong and very courageous.

— *Joshua 1:7*

ROBERT STOFEL

SEVENTEEN
TRADIN' PAINT

*T*radin' paint means racing is close, and close racing is exciting. It's about letting it all hang out with no fear. They fear nothing. The driver that is afraid to trade paint may finish in the back of the pack. Aggressive driving can pay off on certain tracks.

What are you battling today? Maybe it's an addiction. Maybe it's the battle to restore a marriage or a relationship with a child. Maybe you're battling unemployment. Whatever it is, you must be willing to trade some paint and be courageous. Take your problem head-on without fear. Ask Joshua about being courageous in battle. Ask Gideon how he defeated his foe. Ask David how he conquered his tens of thousands while Saul slayed his thousands. Think of Peter walking on the water. He failed because he didn't trade some paint with the winds and waves. So be strong and courageous. Get out of your boat of fear. Walk on water. Trade some paint.

> If [Kyle Bush] can win here, he's probably going to think
> he can win anywhere . . . and maybe he can.
> — *Jeff Gordon*

*T*wo are better than one, because they have a good return for their work.

— *Ecclesiastes 4:9*

EIGHTEEN
GET A DRAFTING PARTNER

Drafting takes place when two or more cars line up nose to tail. The wind travels over the first car and skips the second one, creating a draft that makes the second car suck up to the first. It makes the two go faster. And to win at a restrictor-plate track a driver will need a drafting partner. No one wins at Talladega or Daytona without one.

Scripture affirms this principle when it says, "Two are better than one." But most of us want to go it alone. We don't ask for help. We feel we don't need it, so we think.

Are you encouraging someone in your life? Most of the time we have plenty of people who are downing us or causing us conflict. But rarely do we encourage other people. Sometimes it's hard to find a drafting partner—someone who will push us forward. So be an encourager today. Try to encourage at least two people. You may be surprised at their response. You may even find a drafting partner for life.

> If you want a friend here, bring your dog.
> — *Buddy Baker, on finding a drafting partner*

It is not good to have zeal without knowledge, nor to be hasty and miss the way.

— *Proverbs 19:2*

NINETEEN
STAYING OUT

Staying out under caution is a gamble. Sometimes old tires beat new ones, so teams keep their cars on the track for track position. Other teams pit and take on tires, hoping for an advantage over the ones who stayed out.

Making the decision to stay out is usually a quick one. But most of the time crew chiefs give it a lot of thought before they act and stay out. They follow a predetermined plan—that's not to say it doesn't change. Yet pit strategy is rarely a hasty decision.

We all make decisions every day. Some of them can be life changing. Try to anticipate decisions so that when the time comes to make them, you will act reasonably and not rashly. Sit down at the start of your day and list possible decisions you might face that day. Then begin to formulate a wise conclusion. Thinking through decisions before you are faced with them will give you time to make a planned response. It may keep you from missing the way.

The third time that I thought about it, I was in the fence.
Just too many choices and I didn't make the right decision.
— *Kurt Busch, on hitting the wall*

*I*f you prize wisdom, she will make you great.

— *Proverbs 4:8, NLT*

TWENTY

INFIELD CARE CENTERS CAN MAKE DRIVERS WISE

An Infield Care Center is rarely an ER. Mostly it's a place where every driver involved in a wreck is mandated to go—hurt or unhurt. It's a good rule for driver safety. It's also a good thing because it gives drivers a minute to cool down before announcers ask for comments. It functions like a holding cell. Usually drivers see one another inside. This helps cool a confrontation that could otherwise erupt in front of a camera.

Fans like to see their drivers in a moment of heated passion. Somehow we think it makes them better competitors. But keeping our emotions in check makes us wise. And sometimes drivers fail to prize wisdom. So today if you are mad at someone, if you feel as though you've been wronged, treasure wisdom. Do the honorable thing. Don't let your emotions make a fool of you. Vow to be level-headed. Forgive. Let it go. Make amends.

They name streets after people like that—one-way and dead-end. I like the guy, we play poker together, but if I found him right now, I'd strangle him.

—*Tony Stewart, talking about a fellow driver*

Brothers, I do not consider myself yet to have taken hold of it. But one thing I do: Forgetting what is behind and straining toward what is ahead.

— *Philippians 3:13*

TWENTY-ONE
WORKING AROUND LAPPED TRAFFIC

*L*apped traffic can hold the leaders up. Lapped traffic makes it hard to pass. Most want to remain on the lead lap, so they fight. They block. They scratch and claw to get back on the lead lap. No one wants to be a lap down.

Sometimes it seems like we are a lap down and way behind on accomplishing our tasks. We're struggling to keep pace in this hectic world. We get behind on the bills, behind in traffic. We're fighting to keep our positions at work. But you can get back on the lead lap. So never give up. Don't drop out of the race. You may get the Lucky Dog. Stay at it. God can catch you up. He did it for the Apostle Peter. Peter got behind and denied Jesus three times. Then Jesus came to him and asked him three times if he loved him (John 21:15). He put Peter back into position on the lead lap. Then Peter went out and preached the greatest sermon ever (Acts 2).

If you think you've stopped learning, you're going to get lapped.
— *Robby Gordon*

*L*azy hands make a man poor, but diligent hands bring wealth.

— *Proverbs 10:4*

TWENTY-TWO
MINIMUM SPEED

Every race has a minimum speed. A driver is black-flagged if he can't maintain the sanctioned speed. Slow cars are a danger. It's hard for other drivers to judge a slow car's speed, and they will crash into it.

Life has a minimum speed. If we move too slowly through life, we can become lazy. "Laziness brings on deep sleep, and the shiftless man goes hungry" (Prov 19:15). The best remedy for laziness is setting goals. Goals get us moving in one direction. If money and time were not an issue, what would you do with your life? What would be your purpose? Without a purpose, we drift. We don't stay up to minimum speed. We sleep in or watch too much television. We forget about finishing our education or furthering it. So set some goals. Then move toward them. Never stop dreaming. You will die on the vine.

My favorite part is being at the racetrack. The toughest part is having to penalize or having to react to something like black-flagging a competitor.

— *Mike Helton*

Hear, O my people, and I will warn you—if you would but listen to me, O Israel!

— Psalm 81:8

TWENTY-THREE
FEELING A VIBRATION

Drivers feel vibrations. And vibrations can be the beginning of something bad. A wheel can be loose. A tire could be going down. Something could be about to break in the motor or the drive train. Vibrations are usually warning signs of a problem on the way, and letting them go unnoticed can put the car in the wall and out of the race.

Are you feeling any vibrations? Does something not feel right? Some people call it a hunch. Others may know it as a gut feeling. Maybe it's your health. Maybe a check in your spirit. Something you can't put a finger on. Whenever you feel a vibration, don't allow it to go unnoticed. Eventually it will become a problem. So tackle the issue. Solve the problem. This is what teams try to do as soon as the driver reports a vibration. They bring the car down pit road. So get checked out. Make a doctor's appointment. Go see a counselor. Talk to your priest. Vibrations only get worse when they are ignored.

> I'm hoping that if I ignore it, it'll actually go away.
> But I can't—its gonna happen.
> — *Casey Mears*

*M*oses answered the people, "Do not be afraid. Stand firm and you will see the deliverance the LORD will bring you today. The Egyptians you see today you will never see again. The LORD will fight for you; you need only to be still."

— *Exodus 14:13–14*

ROBERT STOFEL

TWENTY-FOUR
TIRE RUBS

*T*ire rubs smoke. They happen when two cars trade paint or when a driver hits the wall and knocks a fender in on a tire. Sometimes it's incidental contact. But once a driver gets a tire rub, a team decision must be made. How bad is it? Should we pit? Tire rubs are a gamble. But sometimes, unlike vibrations, they will go away on their own.

Life has its tire rubs. The world can knock in our fenders when we are living at such a fast pace. Then a decision must be made. Should we pit? Sometimes if we just wait, the smoke will clear on its own. It did for the Israelites at the Red Sea. God told them to stand still. Do nothing. He would fight for them, and he drowned horse and rider in the sea. The Egyptians were never a threat to them again. When you are cornered at your own Red Sea and can do nothing, let God do your fighting. The smoke will clear if you stand still.

[The car] went left a little bit and then it felt like something broke in the left front . . . maybe the right front . . . but it just went straight into the fence.

— *Reed Sorenson*

When you pass through the waters, I will be with you; and when you pass through the rivers, they will not sweep over you. When you walk through the fire, you will not be burned; the flames will not set you ablaze.

— *Isaiah 43:2*

TWENTY-FIVE
GO HIGH, GO LOW

When wrecks occur, spotters talk. They tell the driver to go high or to go low, depending on where the wreck is on the track. And, as human beings, we would like God to direct us. But we don't always hear him as we should. He seems silent sometimes, and we say, "I wish God would tell me which way to go."

God always leads us along the high road. Yet it doesn't mean the track will remain clear and trial free. But whatever happens, God will see us through. We will not be burned, we will not drown. God is not against you or punishing you when bad things happen. So stay high. Tell him your fears. Give him your problems. Lay them at his feet. He can solve them. He can meet your needs. So remind yourself of this at least five times today. Keep a record. Then shoot for six times tomorrow. Aim high.

I was right behind it, and everybody shot to the left. I tried to go into the grass, and they came down on me. I couldn't really see what started it.

— *Kasey Kahne*

*I*t is God who arms me with strength and makes my way perfect.

— *2 Samuel 22:33*

TWENTY-SIX
HITTING YOUR MARKS

Drivers have their marks. They know where to turn the car, touch the brakes, or accelerate coming out of the turn. Drivers have their own grooves. They know the fastest way around the racetrack.

The Apostle Paul talked about hitting his marks, about running the race that was marked out for him. He recognized lanes. He knew the bumps to avoid. He knew the fastest way was to fight the good fight of faith. He kept steady to the end and received the prize that was his in Christ Jesus.

Has God marked out a race for you? How many years will you live? Will you die of a disease on your fiftieth lap around the sun? Every year we get closer to our finish line. So, today, hit your marks. Set goals. Then hit your marks. Then do it again tomorrow.

I was just trying to stay focused and hit my marks. I heard about a lot of guys that lost their first chance to win a race because they were thinking about what they were going to say in Victory Lane.
— *Jamie McMurray*

Meanwhile, the people in Judah said, "The strength of the laborers is giving out, and there is so much rubble that we cannot rebuild the wall."

— *Nehemiah 4:10*

TWENTY-SEVEN
DEBRIS ON THE TRACK

Damaged cars lose pieces of themselves sometimes. Parts fall off and skid across the track or get lodged against the wall. A tailpipe, a fender, a blown tire. Sometimes it's nothing but a piece of foam rubber. Still, the caution flag waves in the hands of the flagman. The track must be cleared.

When Nehemiah was rebuilding the wall around Jerusalem, the rubble became too much. The workers' strength was giving out because they could not see an end in sight. Their eyes were on the rubble. And this still happens. We see so much that must be done. But our strength is giving out. We've been working hard for so long, and it doesn't seem life is getting any better. Our life is still a mess.

When it all seems too much, refocus. Take your eyes off the rubble. Take it one stone at a time. Don't worry about what's around you. Give your heart and eyes to God. "My son, give me your heart and let your eyes keep to my ways" (Prov 23:26).

I think you quickly learn in this sport that it doesn't owe you anything. I mean, you got to earn everything that you get.
— *A.J. Allmendinger*

A man's wisdom gives him patience; it is to his glory to overlook an offense.

— *Proverbs 19:11*

TWENTY-EIGHT
STOP-AND-GO PENALTY

Serving a stop-and-go penalty is the longest trip down pit road for a driver. It's a penalty that is usually given after a speeding violation on pit road. It's nothing more than a complete stop in the pit box, and then a driver can go back to racing.

Penalties are levied because drivers or teams have taken their heads out of the game. A mental error can cost them the race. So it is with us. Mistakes have consequences. We reap what we sow. So stay in the race. Keep your head in the game. Utilize wisdom. Make it work for you because wisdom offers patience. It lets us know when to stay calm. For wisdom calls out. It's the small voice of reason that says, "I wouldn't do that" or "You need to slow down." And "whoever gives heed to instruction prospers" (Prov 16:20). So listen to wisdom today. Heed its instruction. It could save you from a lot of heartache.

Then a tire went down, and I hit the wall and messed up the fender. Later on, we got a speeding penalty. I was asking myself, "What's next?"
— *Kevin Harvick*

Now we see but a poor reflection as in a mirror; then we shall see face to face.

— *1 Corinthians 13:12*

TWENTY-NINE
The Halfway Point

Every race has its halfway point. The flagman will make a cross with two flags to indicate halfway, letting the drivers know they are halfway to the end. And whatever the Cross means to us, it means we are halfway home. Almost perfect, but not yet. The race is not complete. We still have work to do. We peer through a glass darkly. The world still has its hoarfrost. Pain is still real. Sin is still tempting. We remain damaged people. No one becomes perfect. Not here. Not in this place. So we must choose. God or money? Darkness or light? Peace or madness? This is our dilemma. It's only the halfway point. We are still stranded in skin and bones. "Now I know in part; then I shall know fully, even as I am fully known" (1 Cor 13:12). Until then, we keep racing. We stay at it, knowing that one day we will become more than damaged people. We will be eternal in heaven.

The races I make it past the halfway, we have a good day. Maybe not the day we want, but we leave here with points. And that's really what my mindset is for this weekend.

— *Jimmie Johnson*

When they came to the border of Mysia, they tried to enter Bithynia, but the Spirit of Jesus would not allow them to. So they passed by Mysia and went down to Troas.

— *Acts 16:7–8*

THIRTY
BLOCKING

*B*locking in racing is different from blocking in other sports. Goalies block the goals in soccer and hockey. Football players block kicks. But in racing, blocking is how a driver keeps other cars behind him. And it can work or be devastating. Dale Earnhardt died on the last lap of the Daytona 500 trying to block his competitors. The cars got together at over 180 m.p.h., and a wreck ensued.

Life has its blocks. The way that seems right becomes an impassable route. It leads to destruction, or it sends us in a different way. It happened to the Apostle Paul. The Spirit of Jesus would not let him travel to Bithynia. Instead, he got Troas. His way was blocked. But it didn't mean tragedy, even though Paul was imprisoned in Macedonia. And while incarcerated, the Philippian jailer was saved, along with his house. So don't despair if your way is blocked. God might have a higher thing in mind. Go with it. Let him direct your steps. You might be a blessing to other people.

[David] Reutimann is a good name for him—because he rooted
a man right out of there and sent me up into the wall.
— *Ryan Newman*

But if anybody does sin, we have one who speaks to the Father in our defense—Jesus Christ, the Righteous One. He is the atoning sacrifice for our sins, and not only for ours but also for the sins of the whole world.

— *1 John 2:1–2*

THIRTY-ONE
PASS-THROUGH PENALTY

Drivers get pass-through penalties when a rule is violated. Most of the time it's for speeding down pit road. Think of it as having to redo something you've done wrong. It's a do-over at the correct speed.

Christ offers do-overs. When we sin, when we do something wrong, or succumb to temptation, Christ offers forgiveness. Then we get a do-over. The Bible calls this confession and penitence. Then we move forward and forget the past. We never ruminate because it holds us down. It keeps us from becoming better. We end up replaying our mistakes, instead of moving away from them.

Rumination is never a positive outcome. Cows ruminate when they chew their cuds. Then they regurgitate and chew them some more. It would be like a driver making continuous pass-through penalties when he is only required to do one. So confess, and then put it behind you. Let it go.

This sport has its ups and its downs, things
going right one day and not the next.
— *Ann Schrader, wife of driver Ken Shrader*

*H*ate evil, love good; maintain justice in the courts.

— *Amos 5:15*

THIRTY-TWO
AIR PRESSURE ADJUSTMENT

Making an air pressure adjustment can change the way a car handles on the track. It seems strange how a pound of air can change the handling characteristics, but it doesn't take much. The slightest adjustment can give a driver the lead. It can also cause him to go backwards. Air pressure is fickle.

Maybe your life needs a small adjustment. Maybe you need to tweak your prayer life. Maybe add more praise. Thank God in advance for what he is going to do in your life. It could keep you from grumbling and griping. Being more joyful doesn't take much. So tweak it. Be happier. Smile more today. Don't take yourself so seriously. Maybe you need to decrease your workload. Maintain balance. A balanced racecar drives better. So will your life.

That was fun, maybe the most fun I've ever had here at Daytona.
— *Mark Martin*

*K*nowing their thoughts, Jesus said, "Why do you entertain evil thoughts in your hearts?

— *Matthew 9:4*

THIRTY-THREE
DIRTY AIR

Dirty air is the enemy. It works against every car but the leader. It's the air the leader has used and discarded. Think of dirty air as unwanted thoughts—thoughts that the enemy gets us to think. Jesus called them evil thoughts. He said they were thoughts entertained, which means the thoughts originated with someone else. They were dirty thoughts—dirty air.

Thoughts can pop into our minds. They can originate with the evil one. So don't entertain these thoughts. Put them out of your mind. Don't give them a chance to take root. Refuse them space. The way to do this is by thinking of "whatever is true, whatever is noble, whatever is right, whatever is pure, whatever is lovely, whatever is admirable—if anything is excellent or praiseworthy— think about such things" (Phil 4:8). The moment we turn an evil thought into a positive one about God, the evil one runs. He gets out of our minds.

> This car is just pretty tight, you know, and it really likes clean air.
> It's pretty important to be positioned in the front.
> — *Matt Kenseth, on the difficulty of passing*

*A*fter he had dismissed them, he went up on a mountainside by himself to pray. When evening came, he was there alone.

— *Matthew 14:23*

THIRTY-FOUR
CHECKING OUT

Checking out on a field means the driver has a sizeable lead. The cars in the rearview mirror are more a blur than a threat. It makes for boring racing for a race fan. It doesn't seem like a race if the cars aren't trading paint for the lead. But if it is your driver doing the checking out, then you can enjoy the race. Breathe a little easier. Go get a drink from the refrigerator. Sure, gloating is involved, too. So enjoy it. The next race might be different.

One of the great joys of life is being alone with the Father. Jesus did some checking out during his ministry. His strength for the day came from his solitude with the Father. So, if you are feeling overwhelmed at work, exhausted as a parent, or rejected in your relationships, spend time in solitude. "But when you pray, go into your room, close the door and pray to your Father, who is unseen. Then your Father, who sees what is done in secret, will reward you" (Matt 6:6).

I was driving the car around the high groove and, all of a sudden, the wall jumped out and slapped the side of the car.
— *Dale Earnhardt Jr.*

*J*esus Christ is the same yesterday and today and forever.

— *Hebrews 13:8*

THIRTY-FIVE
PAINT SCHEMES

*P*aint schemes have evolved over the years. Who could ever forget Bobby Isaac's orange 1969 K & K Insurance Dodge Charger Daytona? The pointed cone and the four-foot-tall wing on the back set it apart in NASCAR history. Then there was Darrell Waltrip's 1981 Mountain Dew Buick Regal—the first year of the downsized cars. Today we have the homogenized COT.

Designs change. The constant in life is the nature of our Lord. Even if we are unfaithful to him, he remains faithful. He sits at the right hand of the Father and intercedes for us. He asks forgiveness on the grounds of his work on the Cross.

As we go through our ever-changing day, let us be mindful of our Lord's faithfulness. His temperament toward us never wavers. We have the greatest being in the universe behind us, so don't worry. Be happy. Our Lord is faithful.

My whole vision for [Jeff Gordon's] paint scheme was for that car to look like it was on fire going down the backstretch, like some sort of comet going from Turn 2 to Turn 3.

— *Sam Bass, artist*

You are my help and my deliverer; O my God, do not delay.

— Psalm 40:17

THIRTY-SIX
The Myth of Green

*T*he color green was considered unlucky in NASCAR until Darrell Waltrip's green 1981 Mountain Dew Buick Regal dispelled the myth. Waltrip posted double-digit wins and won the championship that year.

Myths about Christianity abound. Some believe it is a crutch for the weak. Something to believe in because we are not strong enough to believe in ourselves. Those who think of Christianity as a crutch fail to see their folly. Anyone who says they don't need God is living by a myth. Weakness visits even the strong of heart. Life can beat the best of us down. Some just don't have the fortitude to ask for help. Usually we take our myth to the grave. We do it like a three-year-old—"Do it by myself," which doesn't help us win the championship of heaven. "Understanding is a fountain of life to those who have it, but folly brings punishment to fools" (Prov 16:22).

David Pearson used to refuse to park by me in the garage. One day, his team parked his car by mine and he came over and threw a fit. They had to move all the way to the other side of the garage.

— *Darrell Waltrip, speaking about his green Gatorade car*

*H*e causes his sun to rise on the evil and the good,
and sends rain on the righteous and the unrighteous.

— *Matthew 5:45*

THIRTY-SEVEN
A Rain Out

Rain is no respecter of persons. It rains on the just and the unjust. And races get rained out. So don't feel picked on by the world when you suffer. People everywhere are undergoing suffering (1 Pet 5:9). Your coworker is worrying about her bills. Another one is worrying about his children. Others are worried about job security. Maybe they have an undisclosed disease. Who knows?

One thing is certain in this world—it rains on the just and the unjust. Everyone has problems. The moment we are duped into believing that we suffer alone, self-pity enters our soul. Once it takes root, it's only a short race to the place of despair. So remind yourself that you don't suffer alone. Others are undergoing suffering throughout the world. God is not punishing you. So don't succumb to self-pity. Keep your head up. Be an example to those around you. Exercise your faith. Stay strong.

I was looking forward to racing, but then I looked at the Weather Channel, and it didn't look promising. The bottom line is whenever we go I'm ready.

— Bill Lester

*T*herefore I tell you, do not worry about your life, what you will eat or drink; or about your body, what you will wear.

— *Matthew 6:25*

THIRTY-EIGHT
THE BIG ONE

Wrecks happen. Cars get loose. Drivers lose control. And at restrictor-plate tracks, such as Talladega and Daytona, this means the Big One. Fifteen-car pile ups on the superspeedway. Every team worries about the Big One. There's nowhere to go when it happens. There's little room to maneuver when a pack of cars are racing at speeds over 180 m.p.h.

What is your Big One? What do you worry about the most? Money, children, health issues, a relationship, job security? All of us worry that something will come along and wipe us out. It's human nature. But Jesus said, "See how the lilies of the field grow. They do not labor or spin. Yet I tell you that not even Solomon in all his splendor was dressed like one of these" (Matt 6:27–29). When you start to worry, tell yourself it is a futile exercise, and then find a lily. Keep it nearby. When you start worrying, go to the lily. See how it grows. Examine its splendor. It's all God's growth and care.

> You kind of spin out with your fingers crossed,
> hoping nobody else hits you.
> — *Martin Truex*

*H*e is like a tree planted by streams of water,
which yields its fruit in season
and whose leaf does not wither.
Whatever he does prospers.

— *Psalm 1:3*

THIRTY-NINE
ROAD RINGERS

*T*here was a day when teams hired "road ringers," drivers who specialized in racing on road courses. Back in the day, NASCAR drivers weren't fond of road tracks. They could seemingly turn left, but not left and right. And by hiring road ringers, teams had a good chance at finishing in the top ten. But gone is the day of road ringers. Today's racecar driver must race for every available driver's point if he wants to make the Chase for the Championship.

Like NASCAR, gone is the day when a person can work at one company and retire there many years later. Job security is fleeting at best. Things have changed. This is why the tree planted by the water in Psalm One defies changing seasons. It has deep roots reaching to the water, letting us know that God is our resource, not companies. "Keep your lives free from the love of money and be content with what you have, because God has said, 'Never will I leave you; never will I forsake you' " (Heb 13:5).

> I would like to be competitive on a road course.
> — *Dale Jarrett*

*F*or our light and momentary troubles are achieving for us an eternal glory that far outweighs them all.

— *2 Corinthians 4:17*

Downforce is the weight placed on a car when air pressure travels over the body. Teams use downforce to help the cars handle better. But too much downforce can hurt the speed of the car, so there's a balance of speed and grip that every team strives to achieve.

Life has its downforce on our souls. The Apostle Paul said that even though we are wasting away on the outside, there is an inward glory that far outweighs our suffering (2 Cor 4:17). So there is a balance of weight. Keeping our eyes only on the temporal will drag us down. We do this by focusing only on our set of circumstances in life. When things are bad, we are hopeless. We tell ourselves if our circumstances in life would just change, then we'd be happy. But we never are. The key is to strive for knowing God more in our times of hopelessness. This will balance out our lows. "So we fix our eyes not on what is seen, but on what is unseen. For what is seen is temporary, but what is unseen is eternal" (2 Cor 4:18).

I've started the whole process of convincing myself I love this track. My outlook is, I love this place, and I cannot wait to get on track.

— *Jimmie Johnson*

Blessed are the pure in heart, for they will see God.

— *Matthew* 5:8

FORTY-ONE
FABRICATOR

*F*abricators are team members who work in the shop hanging bodies on racecars. They work with metal. They shape and form the body that fits over the chassis. And even though they usually remain hidden on race day, they bring out the best in a racecar—the way it looks on race day. Their handiwork is front and center on pit road, hidden beneath the paint schemes.

The Holy Spirit works much like a fabricator. He works behind the scenes to bring out the best in this world. He hovered over the waters in Genesis and brought form to the void. He's the breath of the Almighty that gives us understanding (Job 32:8). He has been sent to teach us all things (John 14:26). He is our Counselor, our Comforter, the One who can bring out the best in us. So pray today for the Spirit's work in your life, so God "may give you the Spirit of wisdom and revelation, so that you may know him better" (Eph 1:17).

He just passed us. He didn't like make some magic move.
— *Clint Bowyer, on [Kyle] Busch's pass for the win*

*T*he poor you will always have with you, but you will not always have me.

— *Matthew 26:11*

FORTY-TWO
INTERVAL

*I*nterval is the distance between two cars on the track during a race. Usually the interval is measured in time increments, but can be referred to in car lengths. Commentators might say, "The leader is ahead of the second-place car by three car lengths."

The intervals between the rich and poor, the sick and the healthy will always be with us. Jesus said we would always have the poor with us. But this is not a loophole for inaction. We should be closing the gaps, making the poor a little richer, and healing the sick. Jesus did. He told a man to give all he had to the poor, but the rich young ruler was unable to do it. Jesus said we should visit people in prison. Give a cup of cold water in his name. We should pay the worker his wages. It's our duty. We are never told to increase the interval between ourselves and our brothers and sisters. So let's work hard to close the interval. Let's make peace and give to the poor. These are our privileges.

> The whole key to this business is momentum
> and how well things come together.
> — *Bill Elliot*

We also rejoice in our sufferings, because we know that suffering produces perseverance; perseverance, character; and character, hope.

— *Romans 5:3–4*

FORTY-THREE
PIT BOX

A pit stall is the area along pit road where the racecar is serviced during a pit stop. Sometimes referred to as the "pit box." Certain rules apply inside the box—only a certain number of team members over the pit wall to service the racecar, no pit equipment outside the pit box, no part of the car can be over the boundaries.

Rules apply inside the pit box, but once a car exits pit road, the race is back on. The rules change. So it is in life. We constantly move from one set of rules to another. Different sets of rules apply when we are at work or at home, but our character should remain constant. The godless don't worry about their behavior. They don't fear God. They defile what they touch. But not us. We change. We learn "the secret of being content in all situations, whether well fed or hungry, living in plenty or in want" (Phil 4:12). Our character is constant. Our faith secure in Christ. Our hope endures.

I don't know how I'm going to sleep tonight. I'm just sick to my stomach, man, it almost brings tears to my eyes to know that I let the guys down like I did.

— *Greg Biffle, after his pit road mistake cost his team a chance at the win*

*I*n my distress I called to the LORD; I cried to my God for help. From his temple he heard my voice; my cry came before him, into his ears.

— *Psalm 18:6*

FORTY-FOUR
Roof Flaps

Cars were never meant to fly. But they have a tendency to leave the track and fly because of their rates of speed. Speeds close to 200 m.p.h. can send a car flying end-over-end. So NASCAR has mandated roof flaps that were first created by Gary Nelson out of a Happy Meal box. These flaps flip up when cars turn backward and disrupt the airflow to keep the car grounded.

We all need roof flaps—things that will disrupt the circumstances in life, keeping us grounded. So submit yourselves, then, to God. Resist the devil, and he will flee from you (Jas 4:7) because today the devil is scheming. He is trying to send us airborne, make us lose our heads and do something stupid. So make your prayer, "Teach me to do your will, for you are my God; may your good Spirit lead me on level ground" (Ps 143:10).

When I rolled the car 23 times in 1993 at Talladega. That was something I had to get out of my head real quick. That accident helped invent the roof flaps.

— *Rusty Wallace, on his scariest moment*

Your word is a lamp to my feet and a light for my path.

— *Psalm 119:105*

FORTY-FIVE

RACING BY THE BOOK

NASCAR has a rule book that contains measurements and rules for the size of motors and the dimensions of chassis. It tells a team what it can and can't do on pit road. It lets teams know what to expect if a rule is violated. And rules evolve in NASCAR. They change. Some go away. New ones emerge like the double-file restart and the Lucky Dog.

But God never changes. He is the same yesterday, today, and forever. His Word reveals his mercy. The Bible is a lamp unto our feet. It lets us know that "no eye has seen, no ear has heard, no mind has conceived what God has prepared for those who love him" (1 Cor 2:9). So we look, we long, we do as the psalmist and hide God's word in our hearts (Ps 119:11). We meditate on it day and night, so that we might not sin against him. It is our meat, our drink, the first thing we think of when we rise, and the last thing we remember when we lie down at night.

You have to prepare the cars for whatever the rules are.
— *Jeff Burton*

Be very strong; be careful to obey all that is written in the Book of the Law of Moses, without turning aside to the right or to the left.

— *Joshua 23:6*

FORTY-SIX
MAKING IT STICK

Cars stick or get loose. They find traction, or they don't. And on restarts, drivers can only hope their cars stick in the first turn. There's nothing to do but drive it in deep and hope it sticks. There's no real surety. Only hope, only courage. Some drivers are kamikaze. They let it hang out. But making a car stick is more than luck. It's learning to find the fine edge of loose-fast.

There are fine edges in faith. There are things we can do to make faith stick. Daily prayer is one. Running from temptation and soft-peddling anger are two more. Nothing can wipe us out quicker than anger. So begin today thinking about how you will make life stick in the first turn of your day. Faith, hope, and love are the three we take with us into the day. Use all three in some way. Be specific. Vow to love the hard-to-like coworker. Hope for the thing you wait for. Have faith. Believe something good is on the way. Be strong and courageous today.

I was just a little too loose to do anything with them.
— *Jimmie Johnson*

See, I am doing a new thing! Now it springs up; do you not perceive it? I am making a way in the desert and streams in the wasteland.

— *Isaiah 43:19*

FORTY-SEVEN
GETTING A RUN

Making cars stick where they haven't before lets cars get a run. Then drivers make the pass. They seize the moment, knowing it may be their one opportunity. It's not every lap that they get a head of steam. So they pass. They drive deep into the turn. They accelerate quicker on exit.

Look for moments in life to get a run. Take advantage of grant money. Invent the must-have product. Beat the competition. Seize the moment. Don't miss your opportunity to get ahead. What you've been waiting for has arrived. Take it. Opportunities don't come around a lot these days. This is how we race every lap. We keep our eyes open for the pass. "Be wise in the way you act toward outsiders; make the most of every opportunity" (Col 4:5). Look for opportunities today. Open doors may appear. A job offer could come your way. But we must keep our hearts prepared and eyes peeled.

Today, we weren't laying over for anybody. We had nothing to lose and everything to gain, so I raced 110 percent every lap.
— *Travis Kvapil*

*F*or you, O God, tested us; you refined us like silver.

— *Psalm 66:10*

FORTY-EIGHT
WIND TUNNEL

Aerodynamics are tested in the wind tunnel. The tests tell the engineers how well the car travels through air.

Think of the car in the wind tunnel. If it could talk, what would it say about the engineer? "Why the shaking of my frame? Why the turbulence? To what end? I was built for racing." A car could doubt the goodness of the engineer, just as we may doubt the goodness of God when we go through a trial.

Maybe you've been through a tough time. Maybe you don't understand why. Maybe you've even questioned the goodness of God. Experience shows that the turbulence in our lives can make us better, more spiritual, and add to our well-being. We are tested to make us better. So never doubt the goodness of God in a wind tunnel of suffering. Good will come from this. He promised.

Each car has their own style and characteristics, but we hope to have cars matched up aero-wise, so we don't have to constantly hear about rules changes, which is a real pain in the neck.

— *Michael Waltrip*

One evening David got up from his bed and walked around on the roof of the palace. From the roof he saw a woman bathing. The woman was very beautiful, and David sent someone to find out about her. The man said, "Isn't this Bathsheba, the daughter of Eliam and the wife of Uriah the Hittite?"

— 2 Samuel 11:2–3

ROBERT STOFEL

FORTY-NINE
MARBLES

Pieces of rubber from worn tires—referred to as marbles—collect at the top of the track against the wall. It can wreck a driver because it feels like racing on marbles.

We can hit marbles in life. We can care more about satisfying the flesh than maintaining our character. Which is greater? Having faith or spinning out of control? We never stop to ask this before we get our soul into marbles. Stop. Make an assessment. Where would David be in history if he had gone off to war that year (2 Sam 11:1)? Instead, he got out of character. He hit the marbles on his roof. He lost all control, and by the time he stopped spinning, he had committed adultery and murder. And he was never the same again.

Maybe you're standing on David's roof. Maybe you, too, have seen a beautiful woman or a handsome man that belongs to another. Get down from the roof. Stay out of the marbles. It's a slippery slope to ruin. Turn your eyes away.

The thrill of racing and driving the car out of
control with no police chasing you.
— *Boris Said, when asked what he like best about his job*

Wash away all my iniquity and cleanse me from my sin. For I know my transgressions, and my sin is always before me.

— Psalm 51:2–3

FIFTY

GROOVES

Drivers have their grooves. Some like it up high. Others hug the bottom of the track. Everyone prefers different lines. But there's a way that is narrow and another that is broad. One leads to life, the other to destruction (Matt 7:13). And we must choose.

Whatever groove David was traveling to become king, he lost it with Bathsheba. Psalm 51 is his plea for forgiveness. David wanted his groove back. He longed for every word, for a lamp, for direction, for forgiveness. He was broken. He had disappointed God.

Maybe you need to get your groove back. God wants a relationship with you. This is the message of Psalm 51. David wanted God to restore the joy of his salvation and grant him a willing spirit, to sustain him. He had fallen to the depths, into a broken place. Maybe you are there. Ask for the same thing David did.

The track actually had more than one groove when the race was over, to a certain extent. It will only get better, as far as the racing goes, in the next few years.

— *Bobby Labonte*

*I*t was revealed to them that they were not serving themselves but you.

— *1 Peter 1:12*

FIFTY-ONE
RADIO FLYERS AND WAR WAGONS

Back in the day, little red wagons hauled the tools from the garage to pit road. Radio Flyers were the craze. Nowadays, pit boxes are more elaborate. Teams watch the race telecast. They have canopies and elaborate gadgets. Technology changes, and with it, our lives change, the world changes. The war wagons of today will not be the war wagons of the future.

If you could leave behind one message for a later generation, what would it be? Would it be about love, about how to keep a job, about saving money, about how to build and sustain a country? We all leave behind a legacy—something we will be remembered for.

Things change, so leave behind a journal to your sons or daughters. Leave behind something to a friend. Fashion it in the furnace of today, so that later generations can see the heartache and know that they, too, can make it through. This is what the prophets did. They served us. They wrote it down.

That's the best possible finish we could've hoped for with this race-car. I'm really proud of my guys on pit road. They did a good job.
— *Carl Edwards*

*T*his is what he showed me: The Lord was standing by a wall that had been built true to plumb, with a plumb line in his hand.

— *Amos 7:7*

FIFTY-TWO
KNOCKING THE TOE-OUT

Alignment is crucial. Straight traveling racecars handle better and go faster. And when the toe is knocked out, it requires a long pit stop and a piece of string that is stretched from tire to tire to get everything plumb.

Sometimes life knocks our toe-out. We don't run straight and smooth. When it happens, seek realignment. Find the narrow path, and God will direct our steps into the future. "I am the LORD your God, who teaches you what is best for you, who directs you in the way you should go" (Isa 48:17). And this way is narrow. This is why our alignment is critical. Job said, "I have kept to his way without turning aside" (Job 23:11). So stay straight. There are obstacles out there. Keep your eyes on the goal. The way to do this is by giving your heart to God. "My son, give me your heart and let your eyes keep to my ways" (Prov 23:26).

Man that was big. I had just bumped Harvick coming off 4. Smoke came inside the car. I could smell it. All I did was knock my toe-out. I thought [the tire] was flat.

— *Elliot Sadler*

*T*here is a time for everything, and a season for every activity under heaven.

— *Ecclesiastes 3:1*

FIFTY-THREE
A ROUND OF WEDGE

*T*eams take out a round of wedge on a pit stop, or they add a round of wedge. It shifts the balance of the racecar to make it handle better. Whenever you see a crew member stick a wrench through a hole in the back windshield, he is adjusting the wedge.

The way to balance life is by letting go of unproductive things. We stop wasting time on what doesn't work. We stop waiting on things we know will never happen. We adjust the balance of our lives, and it will be a constant thing. Sometimes we have to wake up earlier to accomplish tasks for the day. Each new shift of balance requires time adjustment or a step out of our comfort zone. And these shifts in balance pay off, so keep weighing things in the balance. Then adjust life accordingly. Add relationships that energize you or end the ones that drain you. Do the same with tasks in your daily routine.

I think that I would say that there is a lot of great talent out there, but if they do not have a good nucleus of people under them, they will not be successful.

— *Jimmy Spencer*

*M*oses answered the people, "Do not be afraid. Stand firm and you will see the deliverance the LORD will bring you today. The Egyptians you see today you will never see again."

— *Exodus 14:13*

FIFTY-FOUR
OVERHEATING

Motors get hot. Sometimes too hot, and when they do, water spews out a tube near the windshield. The tube is there to warn the driver of overheating, to let him see the spew, to notify him because nothing is more convincing than what we see.

The Children of Israel needed to see overwhelming proof of their freedom. Pharaoh said, "Go!" once before, but he reneged (Exod 8:32). At the Red Sea, it looked as though Pharaoh would recapture them. But God wanted the Children of Israel to be totally free—not just physically, but mentally. Imagine how they felt watching the Egyptians drown. Their freedom was final.

Ask God to finalize something in your life—an addiction or a bad relationship that haunts you. And when you do ask, be ready for God's action. He will deliver you.

We got some trash on the grill, so we pitted and lost a lot of water and then ultimately blew up. Just by chance, something like a hot-dog wrapper cost us a top-five finish.

— *David Ragan, on the engine failure that resulted in a 37th-place finish*

Wake up, O sleeper, rise from the dead, and Christ will shine on you.

— *Ephesians 5:14*

FIFTY-FIVE
THE CHASE

*T*he Chase is NASCAR's playoff. The best of the best. The top twelve in driver's points battle it out to the end. Only one team is crowned the winner at the NASCAR banquet. It's NASCAR's way of creating year-end excitement.

Why is it that endings need excitement? We begin strong. We are full of enthusiasm when something is underway. Then we lose interest. A playoff system re-creates excitement. Why? Do we need stimulation? Something to cheer about?

It's easy to lose interest. This is why the Apostle Paul told Timothy, "Do not neglect your gift, which was given you through a prophetic message" (1 Tim 4:14). We can neglect our beginnings and move on to other things. Spiritual renewal is a call back to excitement. We remember our great start. We remember our first love for Christ. So revive those feelings you once had.

I wish the Chase was right now because we are in championship form right now. We are very consistent, we are fighting, we are making good adjustments, great pit stops.

— *Jeff Gordon*

Give, and it will be given to you. A good measure, pressed down, shaken together and running over, will be poured into your lap. For with the measure you use, it will be measured to you.

— Luke 6:38

FIFTY-SIX
FUEL STRATEGY

Crew chiefs love to strategize. They love fuel strategy. How far can they make a car go? How many laps are left in the fuel cell? Sure, it's a gamble. Sometimes they just don't know how much gas is left in the cell. The numbers get crunched and measured and shaken together in hopes the car will go the distance. Get it right, and you may win a race. Get it wrong, and you'll finish near the back. Crew chiefs can't control all of the variables that make a racecar burn more or less gas. But the Bible says there is a way to control what we get out of life and to be successful. The Bible says give, and it will be given. Hoarding has never been a Christian virtue. So give something away today. Buy someone lunch. Pay someone's bill. Buy a gift for the poor. Then do it again tomorrow. You will never run dry. It's a promise.

I thought we were two laps short, so I was trying to save two laps, and I just didn't save enough fuel. The guys were screaming on the radio. I guess I didn't realize how close we were on fuel, so I feel pretty bad.

— *Marcus Ambrose*

O God, you are my God, earnestly I seek you; my soul thirsts for you, my body longs for you, in a dry and weary land where there is no water.

— *Psalm 63:1*

ROBERT STOFEL

FIFTY-SEVEN
HAPPY HOUR

*H*appy Hour has nothing to do with drinking and everything to do with drivers being happy. It's a slang term for the last official practice session. Crew chiefs try to make their drivers happy with the racecar. Some get happier than others. Some get downright depressed. They can never get the racecar handling the way they want.

Every day needs a Happy Hour. So establish one hour each day when you will remain happy and not worry. During this hour, make no appointments. Don't watch television. Don't surf the internet. Don't think about the bills. Live as if you have no problems. "Oh," you say. "You don't know my problems." I don't. That's true. But try a Happy Hour. It may be very productive.

Start your Happy Hour in prayer or solitude. Make it spiritual. Seek the Lord as the psalmist did. "As the deer pants for streams of water, so my soul pants for you, O God" (Ps 42:1).

Sometimes you just have to scratch and claw and kick, spit and fight for a win. That's what this whole race team did, along with Kyle [Busch] today.

— *Steve Addington, crew chief*

Sing to him a new song; play skillfully, and shout for joy.

— *Psalm 33:3*

FIFTY-EIGHT
LIFTING

Lifting is necessary. Drivers need to let off the gas sometimes. They back out of a three-wide going into the corner. They know when staying on the gas means a wreck. So they lift to avoid disaster. Lifting can help us avoid problems, as well. Lift when you are about to become angry. Lift when offended. Get off the gas. Let your life drift. Think about your situation for a minute. Get a plan of attack.

Think of your circumstances as having four turns. What can you do in the first turn to keep from crashing? During a race, drivers will lift and get away from the cars around them. Can you do this? Can you put some room between you and the person who annoys you? Then exit the second turn with more room to maneuver. Get on the gas again. Head into the third corner with a cool head. Exit the fourth turn with it all behind you. Focusing on the track will give you an advantage, a place to focus, instead of on the person.

This one is over with, and we'll pick up and go on.
— *Mark Martin*

Not that I have already obtained all this, or have already been made perfect, but I press on to take hold of that for which Christ Jesus took hold of me.

— *Philippians 3:12*

FIFTY-NINE
CAUSING A WRECK

Good drivers make mistakes and cause wrecks. The humble ones apologize. The arrogant ones blame others. It's easy to blame. It's hard to take a good look at our behavior. We like to justify our actions. We convince ourselves that other people are our problems. But really, we are afraid to live with the pain of failure.

Every young Christian eventually sins. It happens. But don't let the devil dupe you into believing that you are somehow beyond Christ's help. The devil tells us if we were really a Christian, we would be perfect. Even the Apostle Paul said, "Not that I have already obtained all this, or have already been made perfect, but I press on to take hold of that for which Christ Jesus took hold of me" (Phil 3:12). And the key to the Christian faith is to press on. We confess, and we try to get it right the next time. We never make the Christian faith an all-or-nothing affair with perfection. Never tell yourself that if you are not perfect, then you are nothing.

When you go into a corner and know you are going into a wall, I would close my eyes because I didn't want to see the wall coming up.

— *Benny Parsons*

My dear brothers, take note of this: Everyone should be quick to listen, slow to speak and slow to become angry.

— James 1:19

SIXTY

BENEATH RICHARD PETTY'S HAT

Seven-time championship winner Richard Petty loves hats. He's known for his elaborate bands with feathers in his hat. It's his trademark, and he is known for this stylish flair. Then there's the cool demeanor beneath the hat that's worthy of a king.

Christ didn't wear hats, but he has the coolest demeanor. Rarely does the Bible display his anger. He got mad at the moneychangers in the Temple. He drove them out with righteous indignation. They had no business making his father's house a den of robbers.

It's okay to be angry. It's a natural human emotion. But it becomes sin when it becomes revenge, when it wreaks vengeance. Notice that Jesus went on to heal the blind and the lame in the Temple after chasing out the moneychangers. So anger and love must always work together. Anger alone is the wrong emotion. "I want men everywhere to lift up holy hands in prayer, without anger or disputing" (1 Tim 2:8).

I actually like the way I am, the role I portray.
— *Kyle Busch*

I remember the days of long ago; I meditate on all your works and consider what your hands have done.

— *Psalm 143:5*

SIXTY-ONE
MOONSHINE DAYS

NASCAR was birthed out of the days of running moonshine. Bootleggers built cars to outrun law enforcement. Then the moonshiners ran their cars against one another on the weekends. From running dirt roads to high-bank ovals, NASCAR emerged. Just as each of us emerges from a not-so-clean past to become one of God's children. We might be ashamed about our past, but the past can be used to create something wonderful. No one understands as we do if unless they have been through the same thing. Maybe you should pray about leading an AA group. Maybe become a Big Brother or Big Sister. Give back to those less fortunate. We can use our pasts to help others understand their own lives. As Mother Teresa once said, "I am a little pencil in the hand of a writing God who is sending a love letter to the world." Be the pencil. Share his love. Redeem your past.

I've done a lot of things in my life, and my history in the moonshine business is no secret. Back in the old days, we learned to drive cars fast because we'd go to jail if we didn't.

— *Junior Johnson*

You hypocrite, first take the plank out of your own eye, and then you will see clearly to remove the speck from your brother's eye.

— Matthew 7:5

SIXTY-TWO

"I Would Like to Thank…"

It's been a long-standing practice for drivers to thank sponsors. Every question the media asks receives a sponsor-riddled response, and it can get ridiculous. But, hey, it's part of it. Without sponsors, NASCAR teams would struggle. Still, it annoys us. It's like a constant drip in the background of every race broadcast.

Whether we are willing to admit it or not, we have our nagging drips. We say and do things that annoy those around us. But usually we only notice it in coworkers or family members. Everybody else is annoying, but not us. Rest assured, at times we annoy others just as much. All of us have our irritating ways. So Jesus said, "First take the plank out of your own eye . . . " Understanding our own faults and annoying ways makes us endearing to others. When annoyed, think this, "How do I annoy others?" This question erases our self-righteousness. The plank is removed.

> Well, to be honest with you, it's not that hard to
> stay positive until you get around the media.
> — *Dale Earnhardt Jr.*

Do not conform any longer to the pattern of this world, but be transformed by the renewing of your mind. Then you will be able to test and approve what God's will is—his good, pleasing and perfect will.

— *Romans 12:2*

SIXTY-THREE
DOUBLE-FILE RESTARTS

Side by side to the stripe and into the first corner. Double-file restarts make it fun for the race fan, even though it is treacherous for each driver. Still it is exciting. Fans like it. We like watching drivers at the top of their game tackle a challenging restart.

Our lives have restarts. We are a people of starts and stops in the land of treachery. We know how to begin and end without finishing. This world will run you ragged. It will take you in a thousand different directions, so resist. Stop conforming. Be transformed by the renewing of your mind. We do this by focusing all of our energy into one direction. Then we become clear-minded. We know how to pray. We discover God's will when we no longer conform to the world's pattern. We break from the past and renew our minds. We hate what is evil and cling to what is good (Rom 12:9). This will eliminate the treacherous restarts after we have suffered failure trying to conform to this world.

I think we will see a little bit different race
for the pure fact of the double-file restarts.
— *Greg Biffle*

Make level paths for your feet and take only ways that are firm.

— *Proverbs 4:26*

SIXTY-FOUR
THE HIGH BANKS

*T*he banking on a racetrack is the height of a track's slope from apron to outside to the outside wall. Some tracks have more banking than other tracks. Bristol Speedway has 36° turns and 16° straights. New Hampshire Speedway 2°/7° variables in the turns and 1° straights. So setups for these two tracks are different. Some build separate cars for different tracks, according to the size of the banking.

Our days will have their degrees of sloping. Some days we hit a slippery slope and slide to the apron. Other days we are sure-footed. The path is level. Jesus said that each day will have its own trouble (Matt 6:34). So we don't worry about tomorrow. It will probably take a different setup than today. Set up your life, so your feet are on a level path. Take only firm ways. This kind of day will give you a great outcome. Strive for it.

You do doubt yourself or how you are doing it, but it does just come down to having the right setup for the car to drive it as fast as it can go.

— *Dale Earnhardt Jr.*

*I*mmediately a rooster crowed. Then Peter remembered the word Jesus had spoken: "Before the rooster crows, you will disown me three times." And he went outside and wept bitterly.

— *Matthew 26:75*

SIXTY-FIVE
BURNOUT

Burnouts mean victory in NASCAR. The smoke, the r.p.m.'s of the engine, the checkered flag in their hands, and the passion. But in life, burnouts means we have had enough. We have gone beyond our limits. It happens when our gifts don't match the tasks we are performing. We burnout when we no longer care or when we are overworked. And maybe you are there. Maybe you are toast and have been for some time. Don't remain too long in this state. You will lose focus and drift into the shadow lands. Temptation always lurks on the edge of burnout. We drift into the place where the rooster crows. Peter did. He denied Jesus and lost his passion.

We act unholy because we have forgotten how passion for holiness once felt. This is why King David said, "Create in me a pure heart, O God, and renew a steadfast spirit within me . . . Restore to me the joy of your salvation and grant me a willing spirit, to sustain me" (Ps 51:10). Make this your prayer if you feel burned out.

I just think that burnouts and doughnuts are OK for some guys,
but they just don't suit me, so I like just doing a victory lap.
— *Terry Labonte*

*T*he plans of the diligent lead to profit as surely as haste leads to poverty.

— *Proverbs 21:5*

SIXTY-SIX
SHORT TRACK PASSION

For Steve Gibson—

Short tracks are fun. The action is fast. Beating and banging doesn't have the same consequences as it does on the larger tracks. We like the close racing. It's the reason 160,000 fans pack Bristol Speedway to watch a NASCAR race. We like to watch tempers flare on short tracks. It adds spice to the competition.

Every life needs spice. We need passion. It gives us purpose. It makes us work harder to achieve our goals. Life is too short to settle for mediocrity. But we settle. We believe we have nothing more to accomplish. Then we add the wrong kind of spice. We start an affair, or we succumb to an old addiction. We cross the line. We make rash decisions that lead to poverty of the soul. But the plans of the diligent lead to profit. So be diligent and obedient when your life feels flat. This feeling will pass if you're diligent. Don't allow your emotions to dictate your decisions. Stay focused.

> I like the short tracks more all the time. I wouldn't have thought my first two top-10s would come on short tracks.
> — *Sam Hornish Jr.*

Do not despise these small beginnings, for the LORD rejoices to see the work begin, to see the plumb line in Zerubbabel's hand.

— *Zechariah 4:10, NLT*

SIXTY-SEVEN
WINNING THE RACE OFF PIT ROAD

Most every team knows the feeling of winning the race off of pit road. Crossing the stripe at the end of pit road first is a small victory. It means no mistakes were made. Everything went perfect— all of the lug nuts tightened, the tank filled with fuel, the adjustments completed. It's an accomplishment to win the race off pit road, even if a team loses the race.

Small victories during the day may not win the race against sin. But they matter. Resisting temptation builds character. "Because we know that suffering produces perseverance; perseverance, character; and character, hope. And hope does not disappoint us" (Rom 5:3–5). This is why small victories are huge. It begins with perseverance. Then character emerges. With character comes hope. We emerge from our suffering with a win. So take it one small victory at a time.

> [Success] comes about because of communication
> between me, the team, and the crew chief.
> — *Ricky Rudd*

What good is it for a man to gain the whole world, yet forfeit his soul?

— *Mark 8:36*

ROBERT STOFEL

SIXTY-EIGHT
STATUS AND WEALTH

Being a NASCAR driver brings status and wealth. Fans want their autographs. They want their pictures taken with them. But status and wealth doesn't make them something better than human. They struggle like us. They may struggle more. Jesus asked, "What good is it for a man to gain the whole world, yet forfeit his soul?" It sounds absurd. Who would actually make this exchange?

Faced with the decision of status and wealth versus salvation, we would choose salvation. It makes sense. It's logical. But we rarely think about it so soberly. We wake up each day and grab for status, for power, for wealth. Yet we never notice. Much like the frog in the kettle. This is how slow and dangerous the process of gaining the world and losing our soul can be. We never feel it until it is almost too late. This is why Jesus warned. It's a daily decision. Happiness is not what we become or possess in this world. It's what we become in the next one.

> It is just a matter of working with what we have
> and make it a little better.
> — *Mark Martin*

---

*J*esus answered, "I am the way and the truth and the life. No one comes to the Father except through me."

— *John 14:6*

SIXTY-NINE
PIT CREW COACHES

*P*it crew coaches help put crew members in right positions and in the correct frame of mind. Some coaches have their crew members doing yoga. Some break down film like NFL teams. Some pump iron. Today's NASCAR depends on pit crew coaches to produce faster pit stops by placing the right crew members in the accurate position on pit road. They're team builders.

At the Last Supper, Christ promised his disciples a counselor, a pit crew coach, someone to guide them. He promised the Holy Spirit who breaks down the film he sees in heaven. He encourages us with the words of Christ. "The Counselor, the Holy Spirit, whom the Father will send in my name, will teach you all things and will remind you of everything I have said to you." So follow the Spirit. As you pray today, ask the Holy Spirit to lead, guide, and direct you. He stands ready to help.

I think people feel that we just show up on Sunday and race, and we just hang out during the week. Most of those guys on the team work seven days of the week.

— *Kevin Harvick*

*D*ear friends, do not be surprised at the painful trial you are suffering, as though something strange were happening to you. But rejoice that you participate in the sufferings of Christ, so that you may be overjoyed when his glory is revealed.

— *1 Peter 4:12–13*

ROBERT STOFEL

SEVENTY

STICKER VERSUS SCUFFED TIRES

Sticker tires are brand new. They still have the manufacturer's sticker on them. Scuffed tires are tires that have a few laps put on them during practice. Teams use sticker and scuffed tires in different ways, depending on a track's surface and traction. Scuffing in a set of tires tends to harden the rubber after they have cooled. It makes them last longer during a race.

God will use scuff principles to harden our resolve and make us stronger. He'll heat up our lives quickly, and then give us an instant solution. The Apostle Paul uses the analogy of skimming dross from heated silver. But as race fans, we can see ourselves as a set of scuffed tires. Our suffering is how God scuffs us in and makes us more like Christ. We share in his suffering, conforming to him in his death (Philippians 3:10). So think of yourself as a set of scuffed tires today. Let God complete the process. You will be stronger for race day.

We had to take two tires. If we took four and got held up in there and came out seventh or something, it would be bad, so we got to restart the green-white-checkered in the lead.

— *Carl Edwards*

*E*ven youths grow tired and weary, and young men stumble and fall.

— *Isaiah 40:30*

SEVENTY-ONE
LAYING BACK

*D*rivers talk about laying back, about saving their tires for a late run at the lead. Laying back cools the tires. The driver knows it's a long race. He must be there in the end. So he's patient.

The Bible talks about laying back. The Christian life calls for endurance and patience. So lay back some. Take care of your body, soul, and mind. Be patient. Evaluate the level of your energy. Never do as Elijah did on the day of his exhaustion. He worked a miracle at Mount Carmel, out ran a chariot, and was filled with fear after Jezebel threatened his life. So he ran from her. Then ran some more, until he sat down under a broom tree and wanted to die (1 Kgs 19:4). But God sent angels to feed Elijah. They made him lay back and rest, which cured his fearful soul. Maybe you need to lay back today. Evaluate your level of energy. Tired souls always long for a broom tree.

Jeff [Gordon] is kind of famous for laying back, and NASCAR has a rule that you can't lay back more than a car length or you'll be black-flagged, but it's usually not enforced, so I saw him laying back. I knew he was going to get a run on me, so I laid back a little bit.

— *Matt Kenseth*

I have fought the good fight, I have finished the race, I have kept the faith.

— 2 Timothy 4:7

SEVENTY-TWO
SEAT TIME

Seat time refers to the amount of time a driver has spent behind the wheel of a racecar. More seat time makes a driver experienced. It makes him better.

Being a Christian doesn't mean you must be perfect to remain in good standing with God. If this were true, there would be no need for confession. So don't feel as though you've failed if you make a mistake. The goal of the Christian life is to grow more in love with people and more in love with God. It's to be known as God's child, as his friend, because there is no greater statement than, "Friend, your sins are forgiven" (Luke 5:20).

Seat time as a Christian is much the same as seat time in NASCAR. Experience makes us better. The longer you fight the good fight of faith, the better you become. So continue to fight by keeping the faith.

It was necessary for me to get the seat time and hone my skills.
— *Josh Wise, developmental driver for Michael Waltrip*

*B*ut the fruit of the Spirit is love, joy, peace, patience, kindness, goodness, faithfulness, gentleness, and self-control.

— *Galatians 5:22–23*

SEVENTY-THREE

SHOCK ABSORBERS

Shock absorbers dampen the up-and-down movement of the racecar. Located near each wheel, shock absorbers are crucial for control. They keep the springs from rebounding over bumps in the track. Think of a pothole on the highway. Cars respond when they hit one. Without shock absorbers, cars would buck wildly, causing us to lose control.

There are potholes in the road of life. There are bumps along the way. Being able to remain steady means we quickly regain our balance. We don't overreact. We don't get hot-tempered or allow our fearful hearts to collapse. We remain steady by allowing the shock absorbers of our soul to balance the bump in the road. And the shock absorber of the soul is the fruit of the Spirit: love, joy, peace, patience, kindness, goodness, faithfulness, gentleness, and self-control. Practice these things, and you will always remain steady.

If there's a lot of body movement, it's hard to control the car in turns, and if it moves a lot when you're stopping, you've got a problem.

—*Ronnie Crooks, shock absorber expert*

*A*bove all, love each other deeply, because love covers over a multitude of sins.

— *1 Peter 4:8*

SEVENTY-FOUR

SAWING ON THE WHEEL

When a driver saws on the wheel, it means the car is not handling. It means that he is violently working the steering wheel to keep the racecar in the groove, to keep it from spinning out.

There will be days when we will need to saw on the wheel of our emotions. So work hard. Keep your life under control. Don't let sin knock you off track. "Let us throw off everything that hinders and the sin that so easily entangles, and let us run with perseverance the race marked out for us" (Heb 12:1). The way to do this is by violently shaking off whatever hinders us. We saw on the wheel of perseverance by never giving up. We stay in the groove. And maybe the groove is staying clean—fighting your addiction. Maybe it's to be more forgiving toward others. Maybe it's being more loving toward family members. Whatever it is, make sure to saw on the wheel of love, for it covers a multitude of sins (1 Pet 4:8).

Once the car got a little bit loose . . . we had to start really sawing on the wheel, it's like it zapped the energy out of me and I started making mistakes.

— *Tony Stewart*

I have set my rainbow in the clouds, and it will be the sign of the covenant between me and the earth.

— *Genesis 9:13*

SEVENTY-FIVE
RAINBOW WARRIORS

For Nana—

Jeff Gordon's Rainbow Warriors derived their name from the rainbow-striped racecar and uniforms of crew members. But before the Rainbow Warriors there was the rainbow. High above. Set in the sky as a sign, as a covenant. God would never flood the world again. It was his promise to mankind.

When you see a rainbow, know that it hasn't been forgotten. God continues to promise way beyond the years of Noah. Rainbows never die. They keep appearing in the sky to remind us—God's everlasting arms are beneath us (Deut 33:27). Promises are his love to us. The psalmist says, "May your unfailing love be my comfort, according to your promise to your servant" (Ps 119:76). He has promised to be there in our darkest moments. He will never turn his back. So we should never turn ours. Maybe you need to promise God you will do something or stop doing something. Make a promise to him.

> Staying calm is the only thing that can keep us
> together and get to the Winner's Circle.
> — *Jeff Gordon*

*B*e self-controlled and alert. Your enemy the devil prowls around like a roaring lion looking for someone to devour.

— *1 Peter* 5:8

SEVENTY-SIX
NEUTRAL

Drivers call their cars neutral when they're neither loose nor pushing. The balance is good. The car is handling, so no adjustments are necessary.

Life can feel neutral at times. No real problems to report. We're not happy or sad. We're just okay. Nothing to complain about it. But don't be lulled into some sin. When things seem okay, we can drop our guards. But the devil doesn't stop. "Be self-controlled and alert. Your enemy the devil prowls around like a roaring lion looking for someone to devour" (1 Pet 5:8). This is why neutral can be bad for us. Remain alert. Avoid places of temptation. Protect yourselves from the prowling lion. Praying the Lord's Prayer is a good way to start the day. Be specific. Pray for forgiveness, then forgive. Ask for protection from the lion.

Just really loose and couldn't get it tightened up. We practice really well and just can't figure out what we have to do to get our car handling better during the race.

— *Denny Hamlin*

Should your springs overflow in the streets, your streams of water in the public squares? Let them be yours alone, never to be shared with strangers.

— *Proverbs 5:16–17*

SEVENTY-SEVEN
RATTLING HIS CAGE

At Bristol in 1999, on the last lap, Dale Earnhardt won the race after spinning Terry Labonte out. Earnhardt said, "Didn't mean to turn him around, but meant to rattle his cage, though."

Some people love to rattle our cages. They enjoy upsetting us. They like to push our buttons. But remember, we are in control of our emotions. Cage rattlers can only upset us if we let them. So take away the buttons. Don't give them a response. Usually this will be all it takes. Fight fire with water. Proverbs says that a soft answer turns away wrath. So never give them access to your emotions. Cage rattlers prey on our weaknesses. So overcome your feelings of inferiority. They attack vulnerability. So be careful what you share with them. It may come back to haunt you. Cage rattlers will use it against you. Don't open the door to manipulation. Stay strong.

I race guys hard. I race guys clean, and I race them how they race me. I think you do have to rattle their cage, but to me, the way you have to rattle their cage is you have to outrun them; you have to show what kind of team you are.

— *Jeff Gordon*

*H*e was chosen before the creation of the world, but was revealed in these last times for your sake.

— *1 Peter 1:20*

SEVENTY-EIGHT
BACKUP CAR

*I*f the primary racecar for each driver becomes damaged from a wreck in practice or qualifying, the backup racecar can be used. But the primary racecar must be beyond repair.

Do you have a backup plan? God had a backup plan. His Son's death on the Cross. He became the sacrifice for us all. Christ's death had been planned all along. God knew his creation might fail. He knew giving us free choice was risky. So he backed it up with the death of his Son. Christ died, so we could live for eternity.

If you feel broken beyond repair, there is One you can go to. 1 John 2:1 says we have an Advocate with the Father. Christ's atoning sacrifice for our sins is the backup plan. So let the sinner go to him. There is mercy. It is new every morning. "Because of the LORD's great love we are not consumed, for his compassions never fail. They are new every morning; great is your faithfulness" (Lam 3:22–23).

Unfortunately, I tore up a racecar, but we have great backups and I'll be out here [Saturday] night, and I'm looking forward to it.
— *Chad Knaus, crew chief*

See, the former things have taken place, and new things I declare; before they spring into being I announce them to you.

— *Isaiah 42:9*

SEVENTY-NINE
BLOWN MOTOR

Motors blow. They break. They stop running. Usually in a puff of smoke. Some catch on fire. The reasons vary. Some drop a valve, and the valve hits the top of the piston. It all depends on the circumstances. Whichever way it happens, there's no controlling it.

Life can be random sometimes. But as humans, we attach a reason behind everything that happens. We say, "If God really loved me, then this would not have happened." So we cast suspicion over the love of God. But God is not a micromanager. He's given us free will, which means random things can happen. It never means that God doesn't love us.

So in the time of our blown motors, in our failure, in the random moments of life, may we cling to the Shepherd. He knows the way through the valley of blown motors. Things will begin again. He promises us a new race. He makes all things new again.

We lost an engine, I don't know why. I felt it start to run a little bit rough down the backstretch, and it broke on the frontstretch.
— *Kasey Kahne*

*T*hen Peter stood up with the Eleven, raised his voice and addressed the crowd: "Fellow Jews and all of you who live in Jerusalem, let me explain this to you; listen carefully to what I say."

— *Acts 2:14*

EIGHTY

The "Pass in the Grass"

One of the greatest passes is Dale Earnhardt's "pass in the grass." His racecar bobbled, and he ended up in the infield grass, but he never lifted. He didn't slow down. He gained control, came back onto the racetrack, and even advanced his position in the race, making the pass in the grass at close to 180 m.p.h. It's one of NASCAR's greatest clips in racing history. No one knows how he kept from wrecking.

Maybe you are at a place in your life where you will either wreck or do something miraculous. The Apostle Peter was in this place after he had denied Jesus three times. He had failed as a disciple. Then came the moment when he stood and preached his greatest sermon. But if he had been thinking about his failure, he would have told himself he wasn't worthy to preach. But he didn't. He stood with new power in his soul. So should we. Never let a mistake hold you down. Get straight and make the pass.

> [Bill] Elliott clipped me and knocked me sideways.
> I was lucky I came back on the pavement when I did.
> — *Dale Earnhardt*

*F*or we do not have a high priest who is unable to sympathize with our weaknesses, but we have one who has been tempted in every way, just as we are— yet was without sin.

— Hebrews 4:15

EIGHTY-ONE
THE DARLINGTON STRIPE

Darlington Raceway is known for its narrow turns. It makes racing treacherous. It makes it hard for the drivers to stay out of the wall. This is where we get the term "Darlington Stripe." It refers to the stripe the wall leaves down the side of the racecar after the driver scrapes the wall in the narrow turns.

The Bible has a lot to say about the stripes on the back of Christ (Isa 53:5). It speaks of Christ's humanity, about how he took upon himself the sins of the whole world, and suffered on our behalf. For this reason, we have a high priest who can sympathize with us. He was tempted on all points as we are. So we can go boldly to the throne of grace (Heb 4:16).

Maybe today you need to go boldly to the throne of grace. Christ will meet you there on his merits alone, not yours. This is why we can go boldly. He forgives sin. So call out, and he will answer. He alone can heal your bruised soul.

> I wanted to see how big my stripe was. You have to
> grade your stripe and I think I got like a B.
> — *Brad Keselowski, on his first race at Darlington Raceway*

When they came to Marah, they could not drink its water because it was bitter . . . So the people grumbled against Moses, saying, "What are we to drink?" Then Moses cried out to the LORD, and the LORD showed him a piece of wood. He threw it into the water, and the water became sweet.

— Exodus 15:23

EIGHTY-TWO
THE BITTER TASTE OF DEFEAT

Defeat is bitter and hard to swallow. But every racecar driver knows the feeling. In a forty-three-car field, forty-two will experience defeat. And for some, defeat lasts for years and even for whole careers. Some never win.

Maybe you have know defeat—years of it. Maybe losing is in your blood. Bad luck plagues everything you touch. Happiness remains just one Happy Meal away. So you've given up on winning. Your temper is short. Rage boils just underneath the surface. Your well of patience has run dry.

Everyone arrives at the bitter waters of Marah. Notice that Moses tossed a tree into the water, and the water became as sweet as Kool-Aid. And, of course, this is a type of Christ. He was crucified upon a tree. Now the Cross is the sweetness that takes away the bitterness of the world. Ask Christ to come into the bitter defeat of your life. He can cause the bitter to become sweet.

It seemed like everything that could
go wrong tonight did go wrong.
— *Kasey Kahne*

*T*herefore, if anyone is in Christ, he is a new creation; the old has gone, the new has come!

— 2 Corinthians 5:17

ROBERT STOFEL

EIGHTY-THREE
FRESH RUBBER

*F*resh rubber is slang for a new set of tires acquired during a pit stop. Keeping our walk with Christ fresh means we exchange old ways for new ones. And this is a constant battle of the mind. Even though we are new creations in God's eyes, we sometimes fall into old habits (Col 3:9–10). We weigh ourselves down with old ways of thinking. We do things we know we shouldn't.

Taking fresh rubber on a daily basis is key to spiritual growth. The mercies of the Lord are new every morning (Lam 3:23). We start each day with a new set of tires. Yesterday is gone. We can't go back and relive it. Some things can't be undone. So leave your mistakes behind. Today is in front of you. Your tires are fresh. Get going. Things will be better if you will let them.

The fuel mileage game is going to be taken out of the equation because you're just not going to be able to stay out on tires without being killed by guys on fresh rubber.

— *Dave Blaney*

*J*esus looked at them and said, "With man this is impossible, but with God all things are possible."

— *Matthew 19:26*

ROBERT STOFEL

EIGHTY-FOUR
CATCH-CAN

Catch-cans have long snouts that open the vent line, so cars can take on fuel during pit stops. Without the catch-can, the check valve—that prevents fuel from leaking out the vent line—would make fueling the car impossible. This is why a second crew member holds the small can at the back of the car during pit stops.

When God works a miracle, it's much like a catch-can. We have certain principles and perimeters that govern our world. We have natural laws we can't change. But when God inserts his power into the world, the check valve of the natural law is bypassed.

Maybe you need a miracle. Maybe you are like the man that said to Christ, "I do believe; help me overcome my unbelief!" (Mark 9:24). Maybe you long to have faith to move mountains. Ask God to pour his mighty power into your life. He makes all things possible. He longs to heal and restore. He can override this world's system.

You talk about a miraculous deal. I really think God put it together because we had no motors at that point, no manufacturer, no driver, nothing. This was a dream.

— *Joe Gibbs, on starting Joe Gibbs Racing*

You, O LORD, keep my lamp burning; my God turns my darkness into light.

— *Psalm 18:28*

EIGHTY-FIVE
A Bad Battery

Racecars run off batteries like a streetcar. And like a streetcar, a racecar's battery can go dead. So most teams have two batteries onboard the racecar. If the first battery fails, they can flip a switch to activate the second battery without losing precious time in the pits.

There are days when our batteries run down. We get weak and struggle to get through the day. But it doesn't have to be this way. We possess a power beyond our own strength. The Apostle Paul says that God will strengthen us with power through the spirit in our inner being (Eph 3:16). We only need to confess our weakness and pray for power. God can strengthen weary bones. He carries us when we can no longer walk. Ask for strength. God says he will never put more on us than we can bear. God always makes a way for the weary. So pray to the One who strengthens weary bones.

You can sit back and feel bad about yourself or whine about everything that's going on. But there's a lot of people in this world that are a lot less fortunate than I am right now, even everything I went through.

— *A.J. Allmendinger*

But those who suffer he delivers in their suffering; he speaks to them in their affliction.

— *Job 36:15*

EIGHTY-SIX
"That's Racing"

"That's racing" is a driver's favorite answer when things happen outside of their control during a race. A motor blows: "That's racing." An accident happens: "That's racing."

When things occur outside of our control, we tend to blame God for allowing it to happen. But life is not that micromanaged by God. God doesn't want robots for people. Accidents happen. Some things are out of our control. Still it is hard to accept them.

When life gets random, never forget that God can bring order to the chaos. Sometimes dreams die, so he can raise up a new one. God can bring something good from every random act. So God will not allow any circumstance to defeat his purpose for our lives.

Don't fret. Do not fear. God is on the throne. He has our best interest at heart. "But you are a shield around me, O LORD; you bestow glory on me and lift up my head (Ps 3:3).

There are going to be people that are faster. We're going to have days when we can't keep up because the car is too hard to drive. Somebody's going to win. That's racing.

— Carl Edwards

But you, keep your head in all situations, endure hardship, do the work of an evangelist, discharge all the duties of your ministry.

— *2 Timothy 4:5*

EIGHTY-SEVEN
ATTRITION

Attrition refers to the amount of cars that drop out of a race. The attrition rate is high when the Big One occurs. Multiple car wrecks can wipe out the field. But attrition can also be low when there are no wrecks and few mechanical failures. So attrition is random. Who knows who will fall away?

Christianity has its attrition. People fall away from the church. They walk in the council of the ungodly. They build their house on sand. But blessed is the man who delights in the law of God. "He is like a tree planted by streams of water" (Ps 1:3). He's unshakable. His roots are deep, nourished by the living water of our Lord. Whatever he does prospers. So stand firm by the living water. Be courageous. Keep your head in all situations. Endure hardship. Stay in the race. Don't become a statistic of attrition.

Not a lot of guys fall out of the race. The cars are built pretty well. The guys that work on the cars in the shop and build the cars and stuff do a great job . . . I don't foresee a whole lot of people falling out of the race, a lot of attrition.

— *Kyle Busch*

*H*e who works his land will have abundant food, but the one who chases fantasies will have his fill of poverty.

— *Proverbs 28:19*

EIGHTY-EIGHT
BACK ON THE THROTTLE

Getting back on the throttle faster in the turns increases lap speed. The longer the driver stays out of the throttle, the slower he goes. Sometimes drivers stay out of the throttle to save gas. The longer they stay out without pitting can turn the race into a gas-mileage issue. Of course, the race has to stay green during a pit window and green to the end of the race. But drivers who are quicker to get back on the throttle win the majority of races.

Maybe you are behind. Maybe your boss wants you to do things quicker. Maybe you have a project that needs immediate attention. Maybe it has been going on for too long. Maybe your spouse wants it finished. Get back on the throttle. Vow to tie up all of your loose ends. Then victory will be yours. Your spouse will be happier, or your boss may give you a raise. So work to your best ability. Put fantasies behind you.

I need something to lean on and feel secure and be able to jump back in that throttle and carry that corner speed—that's what makes fast racecars, and eventually it can win races.

— *Jeff Gordon*

*N*o weapon forged against you will prevail, and you will refute every tongue that accuses you.

— *Isaiah 54:17*

EIGHTY-NINE
OVERTAKE

Announcers say a driver overtakes another driver when he passes a competitor. The Bible warns about being overtaken by our sins. Troubles without number can surround us, causing our hearts to fail within us.

Sin is fun for a season. So we think. Then our sins overtake us, we let them get ahead of us. Now we are trailing behind. Sin leads us, and we follow. Anger leads us into rage. Lust leads us into adultery. Greed leads us into pilfering somebody else's purse.

Sin can become a habit. So keep sin behind you. The way to do this is by putting the Cross before us. When the Cross overtakes us, it leads us to joy, to peace like a river. This is how we know Christ is leading us. We experience the Fruit of the Spirit, so look up this verse in Galatians 5:22. Then choose one to work on today.

We just need to work on finding a little more speed. It's not like we're out to lunch and need to reinvent the wheel. I just need to continue to massage my techniques, and I need to get a little more aggressive at times.

— *Clint Bowyer*

Dear children, keep yourselves from idols.

— *2 John 5:21*

NINETY

JUMPING THE RESTART

*T*he green flag must drop. The lights have turned green. Then the field advances. They go side by side into the first corner. But sometimes eager drivers jump the restart. It's like jumping the gun at a track meet. Things start over. Sometimes the driver gets penalized. So it's a bonehead mistake.

Sometimes we jump the restart. We get antsy. We try to make things happen, instead of waiting on God. Remember the Children of Israel. They gave up on Moses and erected a golden calf. While God was providing the Law for his people, his people were making their own religion. And things were never the same after this. Remain patient. Golden calves look good, but they don't bring about the things of God. They create a false religion that leads us astray (1 Cor 12:2). We follow after the gods of commerce, after worldly pleasure that never fulfills (Isa 55:2).

It was my mistake. He ought to be mad; I would be mad, too. To his team and him, and Tony Stewart and everybody that owns that deal, I apologize.

— *David Reutimann*

*J*esus gave them this answer: "I tell you the truth, the Son can do nothing by himself; he can do only what he sees his Father doing, because whatever the Father does the Son also does."

— John 5:19

NINETY-ONE
IN-CAR CAMERA

*I*n-car cameras have changed the way we view NASCAR broadcasts. We see the driver working the wheel and get a better angle on the wrecks. We see things the way the driver sees them.

Jesus had an in-car-camera view of heaven while on earth. He only said and did what he saw his father saying and doing. He could see and hear what we struggle to hear—the voice of the Father. But we know he speaks. Jesus said, "He who has ears to hear, let him hear" (Luke 14:35). "He who has ears, let him hear" (Matt 13:15). So in a sense, we have an in-heaven camera. We can see what's going on there. If we have seen the Son, then we have seen the Father (John 14:9). When we read about Christ and his work in the world, then we get a glimpse of heaven. For Christ is heaven come down.

Look into heaven today. Do what the Father is doing. You can bet he's not fretting, so neither should we.

The in-car cameras from the late-'80s to mid-'90s was when they really started taking off from a marketing standpoint.
— *Andy Jeffers, CEO of Sports and Entertainment Media*

*A*nyone who does not take his cross and follow me is not worthy of me. Whoever finds his life will lose it, and whoever loses his life for my sake will find it.

— *Matthew 10:38–39*

NINETY-TWO

FOLLOWING THE PACE CAR

Pace cars were made to lead. They lead the drivers to the green flag. They slow the field during a caution. And every driver must remain behind the pace car. If a driver passes the pace car, he faces a penalty. So they follow. They get in line behind him.

Following can be the hardest part of life. We have a hard time submitting. We want to go our own ways. We have evil desires. But there is One who longs to be followed. Christ says we should pick up our crosses and follow him daily. We follow him in his suffering. We conform to his death (Phil 3:10). We forgive our brother seven times seventy-seven (Matt 18:22).

When we follow the Shepherd's voice, he leads us along the narrow way that leads to life. We follow him beside still waters. We make it through the valley of the shadow of death. Who wouldn't want to follow a savior like this? And he is still calling, "Follow me."

I thought he was going to pass. I kind of have a bad habit,
I guess, people call me a pessimist, I think I'm more of a realist.
— *Matt Kenseth*

---

*L*ook at the birds of the air; they do not sow or reap or store away in barns, and yet your heavenly Father feeds them. Are you not much more valuable than they?

— *Matthew 6:26*

NINETY-THREE
PRIMARY SPONSOR

Most teams have primary sponsors that pay for the majority of their expenses. They buy ad space on the hoods, the quarter panels, the trunk. Without a primary sponsor, it's hard to be competitive.

God is like a primary sponsor. He blesses us with the means to pay our bills. He provides. But sometimes it seems God has forgotten his payroll. Money doesn't come in as fast as we like. Yet we can be assured that God provides according to his riches in glory. And God is rich in his glory. He owns a thousand cattle on the hill. He feeds the birds of the air. He clothes the fields. He does all of this with such ease.

Don't fret. "Tell God what you need, and thank him for all he has done. (Phil 4:6, NLT). Then leave it with him. Worry is a sign of distrust. So believe. Let God handle it. He will see you through.

You want to be professional about things when you get out of the car and in front of the camera, but you lead by example through your actions.

— *Jeff Gordon*

But as for you, be strong and do not give up, for your work will be rewarded.

— *2 Chronicles 15:7*

NINETY-FOUR
"WE'LL GET 'EM AGAIN NEXT WEEK"

When bad things happen to good drivers, they know how to put a spin on things. They end every driver interview with a positive statement, "We'll get 'em again next week." It's their way of staying positive. It's their hope. There's always another race on the schedule, another town, a new track, a different cheering crowd. It's their way of saying, "I'll take a do-over."

Do you have anything to look forward to? Will things get better for you? Will you have another chance to race, to do things over again? How we answer these questions determines our potential to hope. So "let us hold unswervingly to the hope we profess, for he who promised is faithful" (Heb 10:23).

Profess your hope. Tell your failures and your setbacks that you will get 'em again next week. Be resilient. Never give up. Keep asking God as David did. "Once more the Philistines raided the valley; so David inquired of God again, and God answered him" (1 Chr 14:13–14).

It felt good to lead some laps. We'll get 'em [next week] at Talladega.
— *Dale Earnhardt Jr.*

I will surely bless you and make your descendants as numerous as the stars in the sky and as the sand on the seashore. Your descendants will take possession of the cities of their enemies.

— *Genesis 22:17*

NINETY-FIVE
Jr. Nation

Jr. Nation is populated by Dale Earnhardt Jr. fans. Some estimate the population as being around 30 million. Numerous as sand on the seashore, like descendants of Abraham. It's an undeclared territory until race day. Then they emerge like a wave in a green sea. They populate the stands. They cheer for the son of the Intimidator.

When Abraham was told by God that his descendents would populate the world, he had to believe it would happen. And by faith Abraham believed. He left his home in search of a land God had given him and his descendants.

By faith Abraham obeyed. He took a huge risk. He got out of his comfort zone. He exchanged ease for a tent in the wilderness.

We never accomplish great things without risking. Think of Paul's missionary journeys. Think of Elijah against the prophets of Baal. Think of David against Goliath. Maybe you need to take a risk. Have the faith of Abraham. Make a move.

I always have fun. I don't really go without fun too long.
— Dale Earnhardt Jr.

I answered them by saying, "The God of heaven will give us success."

— *Nehemiah 2:20*

NINETY-SIX
GREEN-WHITE-CHECKERED

Races can't end under caution, so NASCAR has a green-white-checkered rule. It's an attempt at fairness, at keeping it interesting for the fans. No one likes a race that ends under caution. So the green flag waves, then the white the next time around. Followed by the checkered flag. It's a two-lap finish. Drivers only get one shot at this type of finish. But if the caution comes out, the race is over.

If you had one shot at victory in some area of your life, what would you do to secure it? Change your hairstyle? Take an Evelyn Wood Speed Reading course? Sign up for a Richard Petty Driving Experience? What would you do if you had one chance at victory?

The psalmist prayed. "O LORD, grant us success" (Ps 118:25). Prayer is the best shot we have. Then we do our best to make it happen. We work harder. We keep building clientele. We give more bids. We get competitive. Then the God of heaven will give us success.

> My high was winning the Pepsi 400 in Daytona in July.
> That is the highest high I have ever had!
> — *Greg Biffle*

*B*lessed is the man who will eat at the feast in the kingdom of God.

— *Luke 14:15*

NINETY-SEVEN
AWARDS BANQUET

At the end of every year, NASCAR holds an awards banquet. The championship team is honored and sits at the head of the table. It's their night. It's also a night of remembrance, a time to reflect on the season. The wrecks don't hurt anymore. The DNFs don't mean as much. The season is over. It's a time of celebration.

There will be a banquet in heaven someday. But we will not remember our emotional wrecks. The focus will be on Christ's death, burial, and resurrection—the victory. Our pain will be outdated and forgotten in the new reality of Christ's love. We will know as we are known. The dark glass will have found its light (1 Cor 13:12). We will see through it. We will know what "no mind has conceived what God has prepared for those who love him" (1 Cor 2:9). And faith and hope will no longer be needed—only love will remain.

The banquet will go on forever. The celebration never ending.

The off-season doesn't really come for me until after the banquet. We will have a team Christmas party, and that is when it starts!
— *Jeff Gordon*

*H*e turned the sea into dry land, they passed through the waters on foot—come, let us rejoice in him.

— *Psalm 66:6*

NINETY-EIGHT

SPEEDY DRY

Speedy Dry soaks up oil and any other liquid that is dumped on the track. Sometimes it covers the oil from a blown motor. Other times it is used to dry up water from a busted radiator after a wreck.

God has his own Speedy Dry. He dried up the land so the Children of Israel could cross the Red Sea. They passed through the waters and rejoiced on the other side.

Your trials will pass. One day you will be on the other side of your own Red Sea. You will be healthy again. You will rejoice in the land of the living. God will deliver you. One day your problems will dry up and go away. Your marriage will be healed, or you will find a new job to replace the one you hate. God will make a way for you. He says, "I will turn the darkness into light before them and make the rough places smooth" (Isa 42:16). This promise remains.

Go in the strength of the Lord today. He will not forsake you.

I'm ill as a hornet if I don't run well.
— *Bobby Hamilton*

I know what it is to be in need, and I know what it is to have plenty. I have learned the secret of being content in any and every situation, whether well fed or hungry, whether living in plenty or in want.

— *Philippians 4:12*

NINETY-NINE
RACING THE TRACK

*T*hree-wide racing at Talladega and Daytona can seem like the norm. But try three-wide racing at Bristol or Martinsville and you can wind up in the fence. A driver must know what a track will or will not give him. Some call this "racing the track."

There's only so much contentment that a job offers. We need to understand its limits. Not everyone can be a NASCAR driver or work on a NASCAR team. Some things remain out of reach. If we put too much emphasis on our jobs to make us happy, then we wind up in the fence of disillusionment. Jobs rarely make us happy.

Happiness is a state of contentment that must be learned, just as drivers must learn to race the track and take what it gives them. There will be times when three-wide racing and risk-taking will win you the race. But there are also times when you need to take what life gives you. Maybe you need to be content right now. Ride it out.

The highs are never as high as the lows are low. So you just have to have something more than material things. You have to have some faith to get you through the tough times.

— *Darrell Waltrip*

*T*hen the LORD said to Moses, "Write this on a scroll as something to be remembered and make sure that Joshua hears it, because I will completely blot out the memory of Amalek from under heaven."

— Exodus 17:14

ONE HUNDRED
VICTORY CIRCLE

*E*very driver strives for victory. They want to stand in victory circle. It's the place where dreams become a reality—captured by a camera. This is victory circle.

The goal of every life is to finish the race in victory circle. It makes the moments of past failure fade into history.

The Children of Israel knew failure. They couldn't stop grumbling and complaining. But there were some victories along the way. They defeated the Amalekites, and God told them to write the victory on parchment. God was establishing a reference point, a moment of victory. Eventually they could say, "Remember when we defeated the Amalekites? Remember the sweetness of that victory? If God delivered us then, he can do it now." It was their reference point.

So think back. Can you remember a reference point, some victory in your past? Tell yourself that God can deliver you again.

It's gonna be really wet out here because I'm crying like a baby.
— *Matt Kenseth, on winning the Daytona 500*

ABOUT THE AUTHOR

Robert Stofel served as pastor of two churches in Decatur, Alabama. He spent three years in the inner city of Nashville counselling crack addicts and has spoken to thousands across the southern United States. He holds a BS in psychology and did post-graduate work at Gordon-Conwell Theological Seminary. This is his sixth book and the fourth book in the *Survival Notes Series*. He lives in Alabama with his wife, Jill. They have two daughters.